T0375177

IT'S TIME

to see yourself and everyone

TO LOOK

through the lens of magnificence

INSIDE

PAMELA P. DUNN

Balboa Press books may be ordered through booksellers or by contacting:

Balboa Press
A Division of Hay House
1663 Liberty Drive
Bloomington, IN 47403
www.balboapress.com
1 (877) 407-4847

Printed in the United States of America.

ISBN: 978-1-4525-2163-3 (sc)
ISBN: 978-1-4525-2165-7 (hc)
ISBN: 978-1-4525-2164-0 (e)

Library of Congress Control Number: 2014916592

Balboa Press rev. date: 09/26/2014

DEDICATION

I dedicate this book, this dream come true, to my family and friends. I have learned something from each of you. You know who you are, and I am immensely grateful. Especially to my three sons; you are magnificent men, and I will forever appreciate you.

Thank you to:

My three sons for countless lessons of learning to be a better me.

All the people that have provided stories and situations, as well as being willing to move through those situations.

Megan K. for your insight and the title.

Erin King for your intuitive designs and encouragement.

Lesley H. for in depth editing and encouragement.

All the people that read and made suggestions.

Early on in my personal and spiritual development, I believed that there were only certain people that I could or should learn from in order to become a better person. I am not sure the exact moment this changed, but I do know that I am happy I changed! There came a time when I realized that I could learn from everyone I was relating with because in those moments, that is all that mattered. This expanded my listening, my ability to hear people and lessened my arrogance. I know with every fiber of my being that when I listen, I can learn how to be and how to support. Everyone has something to say that is full of value, and this is true regardless of the way it is presented.

May your journey to look deeper inside yourself lead you to the discovery, the honoring, and the expression of your magnificence. If you hang in there and practice the tools in this book, I'm confident you will experience yourself in magnificent ways.

Blessings, Pam

IT'S TIME TO LOOK INSIDE – to see yourself and everyone through the lens of magnificence.

TABLE OF CONTENTS

CONFESSIONS OF A BULLY

by Megan Knezevic

I was just watching an entertainment news show about bullying. Several times during the show, celebrities, when asked if they could remember bullying occurring when they were younger, said, "Oh yeah. I was bullied." How many times have we heard that? How many times have you heard, "Oh yeah. I was a bully." I don't think I've ever heard that. So do bullies automatically vaporize after high school? My guess is that if we all thought hard enough, we'd find those bullies closer than we want to admit. In fact, when I first began thinking of bullying, I remembered the times I was made fun of for being different. It wasn't until further introspection that I remembered that I was a bully, too.

I can remember my first year of college, separated from my twin sister for the first time. It was our choice to go to different schools to "find ourselves" independent of each other. And I was terrified. I wanted to prove how much I knew myself but in reality, my only guiding light was the idea that I was too cool for my past and I was no longer a naïve, innocent, nice girl. I wanted to be edgy, to show that I didn't give a damn what anyone else thought of me, when it was really the only thing I cared about. So I started bullying my roommate. It may sound like a jump to go from feeling insecure about myself to acting cruel toward another, but that was exactly what I did. One of my roommates, Stacy (aka the "victim") had some unusual habits that made her an easy target for me. At first, I was mostly inconsiderate; being loud while she was studying, that kind of thing. But it got worse. Once, after bombing a test, she put up post-it-notes all over the room, saying things like, "Don't make another big mistake" and "Failure is not an option." This really annoyed me for some reason. Best of all, my other two roommates couldn't stand her either, so we would get together and talk about

Stacy. I decided that something needed to be done. I now had an identity! I would be the person who would be mean to Stacy and do the things my roommates wanted to but were too scared or had too much of a conscience to do. Having a common "enemy" only strengthened my resolve to act like a jerk. So I hung post-it notes too. Mine were written in the same style and tone as her notes, only mine were hung up in the bathroom, and were directed toward her hygiene practices (or lack thereof). Stacy moved out soon afterward.

I was never "caught" for my cruelty. In fact, Stacy never confronted me herself. I never had to answer to anyone about my behavior but myself. Now, thinking about what I did with that experience under my belt, I can see this is when I made even more decisions about my new "identity." I had shown myself that I was not the kind, thoughtful, sweet person that my mother raised me to be. I was inconsiderate and had the capacity to be cruel. I can now see how damaging that was to my psyche and to my incredibly delicate sense of self. I can see that it was the beginning of years of treating myself with disrespect and disregard. I wish I had been caught. I wish I had been mandated to counseling. I wish someone had told me that my experimental behavior, although not acceptable, did not define who I was. I wish someone would have reminded me of my worth.

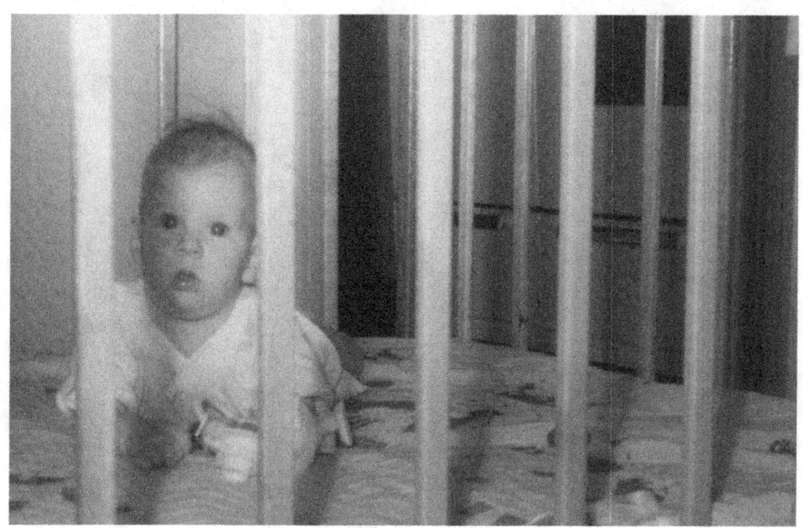

Pam at 8 months. A happy caged bird!

"Love recognizes no barriers. It jumps hurdles, leaps fences, penetrates walls to arrive at its destination full of hope."

MAYA ANGELOU

CHAPTER 1

WHERE DO WE BEGIN?

When changing a paradigm that has been a part of our natural experience, we must first look at the big picture, and explore some misconceptions we may be unconsciously holding on to.

We live in a world where we punish those who do what we deem "wrong," reward or ignore those who we think are "right," and feel pity for (or empathize with) those we identify as victims.

At the same time, most of us don't want to be labeled as wrong. Nor do we want to be labeled the victim. Being labeled the one that is right is appealing, but we know that can't last forever, so when we make a mistake, we blame (even if you blame yourself, it is still blame), we make excuses, or we say we were wronged by something or someone. We even blame our humanness by saying, "I'm only human!"

Thankfully, there is a way out of this whirlwind of opposites—bully/victim; right/wrong; fear/love; etc. The way out is through a *paradigm shift*, a middle-of-the-road ride that cultivates vulnerability or openheartedness and allows you to see magnificence in the face of the opposite. Magnificence is expressing yourself from your core values.

Magnificence and its expression are so much more than that feeling you get when things turn out the way you want them to. Magnificence is also so much more than that moment of experiencing your greatness, although that is magnificent too. Magnificence is that moment when you feel afraid while saying or doing something that you *know* is in your best interest. Magnificence is that moment you feel angry and don't hurt someone but instead treat him or her with firm kindness. Magnificence is also when you feel hurt and you allow yourself to *feel* your feelings from your tender heart rather than only tell someone how he or she hurt you. So when you experience humility in the face of magnificence, you are allowing yourself to overcome arrogance. These are lofty goals requiring commitment, dedication, and a lot of practice.

I have three sons. In their younger years, they experienced themselves and each other as bullies and victims. Now as young men, they are honest with each other and immensely loving toward one another. The process of moving them from the bully/victim paradigm took a lot of practice! It began by teaching them that although they may *feel* like a victim or may be perceived as a bully, that was simply not the truth. The truth is that as loving, thinking human beings, they were far more than these false labels—in this case, bullies and victims. Feeling like victims and acting like bullies was simply an opportunity to learn how to cooperate better and identify what was in the way of expressing their magnificence. Operating like a bully or a victim was not judged as right or wrong; however, it was very clear that nobody felt good about himself or herself as long as he or she was living with these labels. So every time a fight broke out, all of us had the opportunity to reflect, look at what could be learned about ourselves and each other, and then commit to operating differently. We are a "regular" family, so sometimes we did this well and sometimes we didn't!

This way of life requires commitment. And sometimes I wavered in my level of commitment by defining my sons by their ineffective behavior. So I worked hard to develop a deep understanding of discipline as defined by James Hunter in his book *The Servant*, in which he describes discipline as guiding yourself or someone else through a regimen that improves a skill. Discipline was essential and a bridge to staying committed to helping me and my family discover and express our magnificence. This meant I needed the discipline to hold myself accountable to my stated goals with firm and loving kindness.

What does all of this mean? It means that I *can* be a bully, and I *can* be a victim. I *have* been the bully before, and I *have* been the victim. It can be painful to face how we harm others and ourselves when acting like a bully or a victim. This pain usually shows up in the form of fear. Examples may be the fear of being seen as vulnerable or hurting, the fear of being seen as weak, the fear of being seen as mean or hurtful, and many other fears. When fears are not faced—when magnificence is not sought—we resort to being a bully or a victim. We must learn to refrain from acting on aggression—the aggression as a bully or the passive aggression as a victim. This book will offer many different applicable tools for this learning.

The basis of our fears can be summarized in four areas: the fear of not belonging, the fear of being powerless, the fear of not being loved or loveable, and the fear of not being valuable. Most people have limiting beliefs that can be interpreted to meet one of those fears. It is also vitally important to note that these fears are simply limits and are rarely true. This is a key moment in your life because with assistance, your limits can be assessed and moved through, thereby revealing truth and magnificence for you in your life.

Knowing magnificence means there is no need to be a bully or victim and no need to perceive anyone as a bully or victim. Furthermore, there is no judgment on and no justification for acting like a bully or a victim. To cast no judgment, you must suspend your judgment of the person. Separate the deed from the doer. No justification and no judgment equal compassion. This way of being and operating is called letting go—cultivating vulnerability (openheartedness), relinquishing control, and at the same time being in charge of one's own destiny (character).

Now in my fifties, I'm riding the middle-of-the-road vulnerability while bouncing off the walls of arrogance and shame. Comfortable? Not so much! Alive? Yes! Alert? Yes! This is the way to live a life to the fullest, experiencing a different viewpoint of the way our world can work. This is the only place where the paradigm you are currently operating from can shift!

Let's go back to my three sons because I would like to share the story of the time that the bullying and victimhood ended and the "looking inside" paid off with a paradigm shift that has lasted to this day. *Their names have been changed to preserve their privacy.*

I was having dinner at a friend's house. All three boys were hanging out at home together. They didn't get to do this very often, as they were still young, yet they loved the freedom of being by themselves for a few hours. Let me introduce John, Mark, and Tom.

I was gone for about one and a half hours when I received a phone call from John. I could hear a lot of chaos in the background, and John was frantic. He was very difficult to understand, but thank goodness for my upbringing and my ability to remain calm in the face of a storm. He frantically shared that a fight had broken out. Mark was waving sharp knives and threatening John and Tom while chasing them around the house. John was outside and was frightened because Tom was still inside with Mark. John was convinced that Mark intended to act on his threats. My advice was to stay outside and, most importantly, no more fighting. And if he was that afraid, he should go to the neighbor's house. I said good-bye to my friends and headed home. I was initially disappointed and annoyed that I was having to cut a fun evening short. I also realized quickly that that attitude would not serve them, the situation, or me.

I knew my ride home would need to be used wisely because there would be a lot of blaming when I got home. I reflected on each one of the boys, remembering how much I love and appreciate them. I focused on their strengths and remembered the times when they enjoyed each other. It is true that I had to resist the urge to hang on to the resentment I felt around their role in ruining my night with my friends!

When I arrived home, John and Tom were in the living room, watching a movie. Mark was in his bedroom. I called Mark to join the rest of us in the living room and turned off the television. I announced that we would be talking and working through this issue. I also stated that we would stay with this as long as it took because I felt it was time for us to "hang in there" together and they were now old enough; they knew enough to make stronger commitments to each other. I took the rolling eyes and heavy sighs as a good sign because it meant they were taking me seriously!

I began by stating the rules. I told them they would each get a turn to share their side of the story, and when sharing, there would be no cross talking or defending from anyone else. This was my chance to listen deeply.

Each of them shared. I found their stories interesting because none of them were taking responsibility. Most of the blame was being placed on the bully in the situation, Mark, who was justifying his behavior by saying he was being bullied by John and Tom.

Now, as you are reading this, you may be remembering fights you've witnessed or have engaged in. Also, note that this is a smaller scale conversation that customarily happens during street fights, gang wars, police standoffs, religious wars, and world wars. You see, I noticed the same thing, and it brought tears to my eyes.

John asked me why I was crying. I explained what I was realizing. My tears increased as I told them how sad this was making me feel because I knew how much they loved each other. I described how they have to close off their hearts as well as suspend their love for each other in order to express so much anger toward one another and how scared they must be to resort to behavior unlike their true nature. As I finished sharing, all three of them had tears in their eyes and were visibly shaken. **It was as if a light bulb had turned on and their hearts opened to the truth of the situation from a more expanded view.**

I asked Tom what he was feeling. By the way, I asked him first because he was showing the most emotion. He shared vulnerably and admitted how scared he was of Mark and how scared he gets all the time when Mark gets mad at him. He then revealed how he understands why Mark gets mad because he (Tom) is mean to him, makes fun of him, and then gets John to join in. I get tears in my eyes now when remembering this precious moment. Tom's sharing opened up a whole new level of relating for the three of them. It allowed Mark and John to connect with their feelings on a deeper level, feel safe expressing their feelings, and acknowledge their responsibility for starting and fueling the fight.

After I knew they all felt they had been heard, I asked each of them how they felt. The consensus was "much better!" I then asked what each of them wanted. Tom started and looked directly at his brothers and said, "I want us to stop being so mean to each other." I loved this because the reality was that they would most likely "fight" again, yet they did not have to be mean to each other even though they may disagree. John and Mark agreed that they wanted the same thing. I then asked them to verbally commit to each other to no longer be mean to one another. They did this by looking each other in the eyes, addressing each other by name, and stating their commitment to not being mean. Everyone hugged and we went out for ice cream to be together as a family!

Since the commitment was made, it set the stage to remind each other in the future of the commitment if it was ever broken (and it was). However, they were kinder to each other, worked through disagreements quicker, and were more compassionate.

I hope you enjoy reading *It's Time to Look Inside*, and remember that through the process of discovery, honoring yourself and others, and expressing your magnificence, you will be able to treat others and yourself with more compassion, and see others and yourself as brilliant. This is the richness the world—and you—deserve to experience.

Pam, her Mom and 6 siblings. We really like each other!

"Yes, I am imperfect and vulnerable and sometimes afraid, but that doesn't change the truth that I am also brave and worthy of love and belonging."

BRENE' BROWN
The Gifts of Imperfection

CHAPTER 2

THE DEFINITIONS

Who is the bully? What is a victim? Here I'll explore each role, and develop a cohesive definition to use as a reference point throughout the book. I will also illustrate what is meant by "looking inside." Remember: We operate as a bully or a victim as long as we view someone else as a bully or a victim.

Bully – a person who likes to hurt or intimidate those weaker than himself, to coerce by threats, to intimidate (Webster's Dictionary definition).

Victim – a person injured or killed by circumstances or people who are beyond his control (Webster's Dictionary definition).

It's easy to see with these definitions that I would certainly rather be a victim than a bully, *and* I prefer neither! How about you? Incidentally, I disagree with both definitions because the bully is automatically the assumed "bad" person because they "like to hurt or intimidate," and the victim is not in control!

I do believe the bully is threatening, hurtful, and intimidating. I do believe the victim is injured or killed by circumstances or others. But I also believe that the bully does not necessarily *like* to threaten, hurt, or intimidate, and the victim is not necessarily out of control, even though it may *feel* that way. In both definitions (and remember we are talking about people here) there is nothing empowering. The bully is not empowered to feel differently or see things differently because the assumption is that he/she likes it. The victim is not empowered to change their circumstances because they are out of their control.

Empowerment comes from feeling, knowing, and experiencing the responsibility of creating what one truly desires. A bully would only desire to threaten, hurt, or intimidate if they believe there are no other options. A victim would be resigned to maintaining a victim status if they believed there was no way to be in control of the circumstance.

Whatever we buy into (bully or victim mindset) we practice. If you believe the kid at school was a bully to another kid, you have no other choice but to practice and operate from the bully/victim mindset paradigm. Yet, if you believe the kid at school was only acting mean because he is not in service to his/her magnificence, then you practice and operate beyond that paradigm. I suggest the latter!

Before I go further on this topic, let's understand what I mean by "look inside." To *look inside* means to discover *your* beliefs, *your* thoughts, and *your* feelings. To *look inside* means you will discover and acknowledge how you want to be treated, how you want people to see you, and how you want to treat others. To *look inside* means you will go on a journey to discover the gap between what you say you want and what you actually get and who you say you want to be and who you actually express yourself to be. To *look inside* means to acknowledge to yourself that we all have the capacity to change, *and the only effective way to change is to look inside.*

Each one of us has resorted to bullying before. It is painful to face how we harm others and ourselves when acting like a bully. Yet, to look inside will help you see yourself in the bully role and enable you to understand why others react the way they do. It doesn't mean you condone it—it means that you become the equal that can approach the bully with compassion rather than approaching the bully as a bully.

Each one of us has felt like the victim before. In those moments we feel powerless. Since no one enjoys or would actually decide to feel powerless, *looking inside will help you discover a new way to be responsible beyond your perceived limits.*

Each time you respond to someone by thinking it's their fault you feel the way you feel, you are placing yourself in the position of the bully/victim paradigm. **You are being a bully when you are**

blaming and a victim by declaring that someone else is making you feel a certain way. This is a new and empowering way of looking at things, and from this new perspective you can begin to make the necessary paradigm shift. That shift can occur only when you are compassionate enough with yourself to take an honest look inside. By looking inside you may uncover and unravel things that will be initially unpleasant, yet freedom awaits—the freedom of your brilliance, your innate magnificence—which is difficult to see in yourself or others when you are engaged in validating the belief that you or others are bullies and/or victims.

On a family vacation we were watching some videos on my sister's camera of her young children (there were about fifteen people in the room). Brian, who was six years old, was so cute in the video, and we were all laughing. Suddenly, Brian ran into the room extremely upset that we were "laughing at" him. He immediately ran up to his Mom and started hitting her. I was sitting next to her. It was a perfect display of the moment when we decide we are a victim and instantly become a bully. What happened next was even more perfect. His mom gently and firmly picked him up and took him in the other room. She did this without yelling at him or acting hurt by his behavior. When they came out of the bedroom about five minutes later, she was holding him, and he was smiling. They sat back down and I asked her what she did. She held him until he calmed down and then simply explained to him that our laughter was because of how much we were enjoying him, and he just misunderstood us. She explained until he completely understood, then he apologized for hitting her and hugged her.

I believe this is the way all "bullies" start out feeling—they actually feel like a victim of something or someone and then act out in order to overcome those victim feelings. In other words, acting like a bully is really acting like an angry victim! Also, in most circumstances, the perceived victim feels victimized because they don't know how to respond and usually don't have all the information.

Our family at a time when looking good helped us feel good.

"If you think the people you attract could be better, then it's time for you to improve yourself."

JOHN C. MAXWELL

CHAPTER 3

INTENTION & COMMITMENT

Yes, it's chapter three, but this is the very beginning of a life-long process that begins with the power of intention, the initiative of commitment, and some Silent Space, and ends with the initiative of commitment driven by a longing deep inside oneself.

When we are ready to make a change, there is a pivotal moment when we make a commitment. The moment we pause to realize and recognize that we are reviewing a situation in the context of there being a bully or victim, is the moment when the world is open to us and the moment when there is breathing room to truly be in the present moment. This is the moment when you are taking the time to freely respond from your magnificence.

However, we all know that pausing is a great idea, and we often do not pause in the "heat" of a situation. So the learning may first occur when you step away from a situation and decide to look at it to see what can be done differently should this arise again. You can also begin a proactive approach through **first being committed to not harming anyone with your words or actions**—making this the basis of your magnificent life.

"Great idea, impossible to accomplish," is what I often hear when making this suggestion. I agree with that! This means we are going to have something that will challenge us throughout life and give us opportunity after opportunity to practice and practice and get better and better. Every time you practice, every time you have a success, every time you fail and re-commit is an indication that you are in service to your magnificence.

If you choose to have an intention to not harm with your words or actions, then to be committed, it means that you are dedicated to that intention. Your commitment can be measured by considering the results that your commitment has produced. You see, we are always committed to something. A very popular phrase is, "I have commitment issues or problems." This is a basic lie we tell ourselves. We usually don't have a commitment issue or problem. The problem is that we are not paying attention to what we are committed to. Think about this: If I say I am committed to do no harm with my words or actions, and I am sarcastic and hurtful to someone, telling them that it wasn't my *intention* and telling myself I have commitment issues, lets me relinquish responsibility for my actions. By claiming a victim mindset, it stops you from learning anything, lets you give up on yourself, therefore your magnificence.

The best way to be in service to your magnificence is to measure commitment in levels. This will give you the greatest opportunity for adjustment and learning. On the following pages is a chart developed as a tool for commitment measurement. Don't use this information to define yourself or others as "right" or "wrong" based on a level of commitment. Instead, use it to measure yourself or to assist others in operating from a level of commitment that is more fulfilling. Look at the chart now before continuing.

INTENTION = RESULTS. HOW TO CREATE THE RESULTS YOU INTEND

When you state your intention and decide on a level of commitment, you may find yourself not accomplishing what you stated. Understanding what is causing the gap between what you *say* you want and what you *get* is simple when you recognize that it's *you* that's sabotaging your ability to accomplish the intended result, rather than it being *someone else's* fault (which implies *blame* rather than *responsibility*). **While it may be easier to believe that someone or something else has caused you to fail, you will learn the most (and grow as a human being) from looking inside yourself.**

LEVELS OF COMMITMENT

FULFILLING COMMITMENTS

Intention Focused On:	Example	Attitude Expressed	Attitude Required for Higher Level
Improving the World	"I am consciously living from a commitment that is focused on being of service to a Source greater than myself."	A knowing that what you do is part of something bigger. You understand that your actions impact more than you are aware of.	A faith that the universe works even though you don't understand the purpose of your contribution. I know that to harm one is to harm all, and to love one is to love all.
Improving the Community	"I want our town to be a great place to live. I love where I live and engage with my neighbors, or religious community or school."	Interest in the wellbeing even of those who do not directly contribute to you.	The desire to have the world come together as one. Create and support a vision of global oneness.
Being a Team	"I commit to the task, its purpose, and to the individual fulfillment of each member of the group."	A willingness to either lead or support the leader. Recognition that putting the group goal first meets your personal goals.	Develop a sincere appreciation for the people who love to do tasks that you dislike doing. Engage in a search for people who are better than you.
Being a Family/ Couple	"I commit to the task, its purpose and to the individual fulfillment of each member of the group."	Seeing your family/ partner as yourself and allowing them to be themselves. Loving them through perceived mistakes.	Overcome your need to be against some outside group in order to achieve closeness in your group. Overcome your need for judgments.
Being a Friend	"I will only do what is a reflection of who I really want to be, focusing on preferences rather than requirements."	The courage to allow someone to see you without facades. Accepting yourself with your faults and loving them with their faults.	Being friendly for the purpose of expanding your awareness of your oneness and your spirituality instead of for personal satisfaction.
Task Satisfaction/ Personal Gain	"I want to do a good job. I want to earn enough money so that I never have to postpone expressing myself."	You have faith in your ability to do and learn. You get your joy from doing. An interest in others and the willingness to choose to be useful instead of being petty or prideful.	Overcome your need for perfection, replacing it with working toward steady improvement. Adopt the goal of using your desires to inspire yourself to be more useful.

LESS FULFILLING COMMITMENTS

Intention Focused On:	Example	Attitude Expressed	Attitude Required for Higher Level
Proving Yourself	"No matter what I do it is never enough." A desire to be better than others or special. A need to prove that you are OK or powerful or doing enough.	Striving for superiority. Comparing. Defensiveness. Doing things for approval. The need to be special. Be a favored one.	Do anonymous acts of service. Get your fulfillment from the joy of contribution, rather than from the acknowledgment. Search for the value of others and yourself, and then tell them and yourself.
Protest	Feeling that, "others have the power." Under-estimating the effect you have on others. "I will not, and you can't make me." Being late or not returning calls, emails or texts.	Being on strike. Pleasing. Complaining. Dwelling on injustices. Acting like you don't care.	Take action on what you can do to improve upon the situation. Willingness to be responsible.
Survival	"I've got to take care of myself. I must make sure I get what I need."	Desperation. Seeking personal comfort over taking the risk you would like to. Worry about getting your share.	Remind yourself that you can handle whatever happens.
Revenge	Actions with the intent to hurt others or actions disguised as noble that end up hurting others. Sarcastic remarks. Angry or "cutting" words. Fighting back.	They hurt me first. Who cares. They must learn a lesson. "They deserve the punishment they are getting."	Instead of getting even, quit the battle while the other person is ahead.

When we have an intention (or say we want something) we immediately begin the process of "going for it." Sometimes when we don't get it, we may tell ourselves it was the wrong thing to want, or we begin blaming others for why we don't have it. The following diagram may help you see how you don't necessarily need to change what you want, or blame anyone, because what really happened is that something else you don't recognize got in the way of you achieving your stated goal.

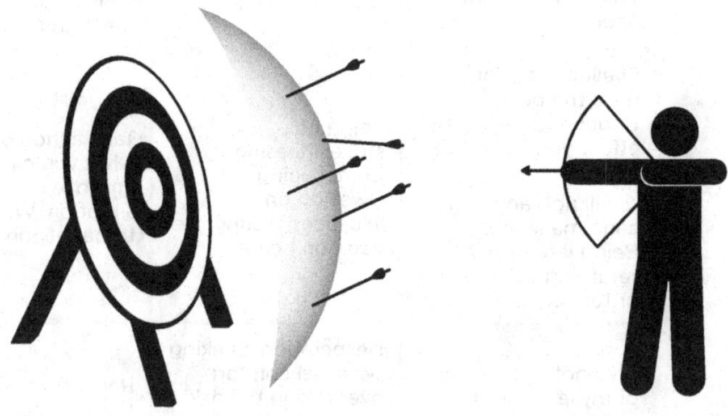

Most of the time when we don't get the results we want, there is a subconscious (or unrecognized) motive to recognize. Knowing this simply means it is time to look within (inside). Well beneath our subconscious motive lies our magnificent self. We don't see it sometimes because we have put up a protective layer. You can use any tip received in this book to help you look inside.

When you don't get the results you want, first you must cultivate the ability to recognize you are off track from accomplishing the results. After that, you can use the Commitment Chart and several other resources you'll find in this book as helpful tools.

EXPANDING CURIOSITY AND LEARNING FROM EVERYTHING

In order to increase curiosity and your ability to learn from experiences, we all need to cultivate the skill of listening to ourselves (or our inner thoughts) rather than listening to what we are constantly telling ourselves.

This tool is called the Silent Space. It inspires curiosity and listening, which opens the door to let you decide how you want to proceed. In the context of this book, your choice is to use the **Commitment Chart** to change your level of commitment, or use the **Cycle of Limiting Belief Creation** tool (explained later) to enable you to change a limiting belief to a new, more expanded belief. You may also decide to choose to use both tools.

The Silent Space is the space (or moment) you take to *respond* rather than *react*. The purpose of the Silent Space is to increase your curiosity and your ability to learn from any experience. Actually, you are already using this tool in your daily life. The next section will just teach you how to use it more consciously and effectively.

Most people want to communicate from their positive characteristics. Unfortunately, when communication gets challenging, our most admirable characteristics are the first thing to fly out of the window! It may seem like the reason you "lose your cool" is because the other person isn't being reasonable, is arguing, or is impeding the process in some way. I won't dispute that the other person may have a role in disrupting the way you want the conversation to go. However, this tool will empower you to operate within your stated values and goals, even when the other person does not.

Paul Tough, researcher and author of *How Children Succeed*, says, "*Two of the most important executive functions are cognitive flexibility and cognitive self-control. Cognitive flexibility is the ability to see alternative solutions to problems, to think outside the box, to negotiate unfamiliar situations. Cognitive self-control is the ability to inhibit an instinctive or habitual response and substitute a more effective, less obvious one.*"

Viktor Frankl was an Austrian neurologist and psychiatrist as well as a Holocaust survivor. His book, *Man's Search for Meaning*, chronicles his experiences as a concentration camp inmate and describes his method of finding meaning and thus a reason to continue living. One of his famous quotes is: "*Between stimulus and response there is a space. In that space is our power to choose our response. In our response lies our growth and our freedom.*"

So in any situation or conversation, we have a stimulus that triggers our response and an opportunity to consciously create a space between the stimulus and the response. Sometimes that space is very narrow, and sometimes that space is wider. When the space is narrow (or you are responding immediately) it may be because you are protecting yourself from something, or responding with defensiveness, anger, or withdrawal. You can see how this type of response could leave you blaming or making excuses for your behavior. This is called being in *protection*. For example, you will respond very quickly saying things like, "I didn't mean that," or "I'm not mad, you are!", or "No I didn't." It is during these interactions that you'll later notice you may regret what you said, or wish you would have said something more effective. This is an excellent opportunity to recognize that the Silent Space was narrow, and you were most likely not operating from your magnificent self.

Shifting from being in protection to being in learning will help you increase the Silent Space. **When you increase the Silent Space, you create time to stop, analyze, decide, and choose your responses in a way that requires you to be responsible for your actions.** This way is usually anchored in your magnificent self. In the *learning* state, you express a desire to discover more about yourself as well as a desire to learn from and about others. Whereas in the *protection* state we hide our shortcomings or our true feelings, and instead give off the appearance that we already know, which leaves no room for self-discovery. Getting to know yourself better enables you to develop more curiosity. And when you do this, you'll grow, learn, and develop the capacity and desire to be more compassionate.

Increasing the Silent Space creates a bridge that allows more time rather than creating a wedge that builds resentment.

Think of a time when you felt like you were being treated in a way that left you feeling victimized, or a time when you would have been called the bully in a situation because of how you reacted.

I recall a time when I was being made fun of in the fifth grade by some of my classmates. I certainly felt victimized by them. I remember how I immediately protected myself with a tactic I catch myself using to this day. I laughed when they were making fun of me, and I even joined in, exaggerating what they were saying. On the outside this looked like it didn't bother me, and I also believe this was an excellent coping mechanism. This became my protective behavior—protecting myself from acknowledging how I truly felt, and protecting myself from expressing my truth. However, as I learned to pause to increase the Silent Space, I began to see that I had developed a deep-seated belief that I am that person: ugly, fat, unattractive, stupid, a loser. I have spent a good twenty-five years attempting to dispel these beliefs about myself. It took increasing the Silent Space (pausing before responding) to recognize how I was operating from a limiting belief about myself. When I dispel the limiting belief, I expand my curiosity and respond from my magnificent self. Imagine the difference in the type of response—believing I'm unattractive or believing I'm beautiful.

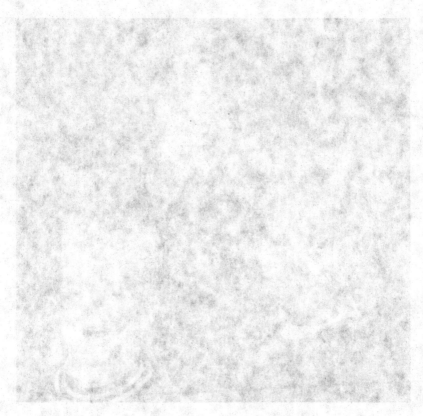

My teachers and a joy in my life

"Children are constantly gathering information through nature, teachers, prayers, intuition, family and friends. They are curious. Have you noticed how often children ask the question, Why? or How Come? They love to learn."

SUSIE WALTON

CHAPTER 4

THE FOUR BASIC NEEDS

Your basic needs must be answered and fulfilled so you may avoid the bully/victim paradigm and so you may stop acting as the bully or the victim if that already exists in your life, and instead live from your magnificence. Let's discover how to fulfill these essential, life-sustaining needs.

It's important to know the **four basic needs** before you learn to move beyond your limiting beliefs. **They are: the need to be loved, the need to belong, the need to feel powerful, and the need to be valuable.** If any of these four basic needs are not being met, you will resort to ineffective behavior, such as bullying or behaving based on feeling like a victim.

THE NEED TO BE LOVED

The need to be loved unanswered can be seen in a parent becoming upset because their child has done something they disapprove of. This perceived lack of acceptance of the child from the child's perspective starts the chain reaction of believing that they are unlovable because they don't receive an "A" on a report card, or strike out in a baseball game, or miss the goal in a soccer game, or fight with a sibling. As soon as this perception takes hold, many things occur such as, blaming, pushing back, proving themselves, or sulking—all basic bullying or victim responses.

We do *not* get the love we deserve! We let ourselves receive the love we *think* we deserve. The victim of a bully does not think they deserve much love based on the results of the interaction. Let me begin this story by telling you that my sons are best friends now that they are young adults, however, they still have disagreements. John and Tom liked a lot of the same things, like sports, television shows, and music. Mark didn't like sports very much, enjoyed completely different television programs, and did not like the music his brothers enjoyed. We had the agreement that whoever was in the front seat of the car on a ride or trip got to be in charge of what played on the stereo. One day, John was in the front seat and promptly put in one of his new CD's. John and Tom began singing and commenting on how great the music was.

Mark immediately began berating and making fun of the music, as well as putting down John and Tom for the type of music they liked. This began a firestorm of name calling which quickly got out of hand and ugly! It is not a time to clearly identify the perceived bully or victim because they were all operating from both. What is valuable to see here is that Mark was the first to be upset and hurt, claiming that they "gang up" on him because they don't like him. In that moment he felt he was the perceived victim and did not think he deserved love from his brothers because he disagreed with their choice in music.

The bully does not think they deserve much love based on the way others feel about him or her. With John and Tom being the perceived bullies in that moment, they did not believe their brother loved them because of how he was berating them.

I also remember a time when I was working with a mother and daughter. The mother said, "I want you to know how much I love you!" The daughter's response was, "I know you love me, I just don't think you show it much!" The expression of the love is the key! The truest test to the expression of love is in the face of someone acting in a way that would make it difficult to show them love. This is what the daughter was saying—she felt loved when she was "good," and not loved when she was acting out. John and Tom could have expressed their love and care for Mark in the moment he began berating their music. He was clearly acting in a way that made it difficult to show him love, yet expressing love to him would have been the key to helping him feel accepted and part of the team whether they had the same taste in music or not.

For both the perceived victim and bully, it will be important to focus on *your* love of their inner strength and magnificence, and at the very least, seek to discover it.

Fulfill the need to be loved by acknowledging the places in your life where you are loved and where you love. You can start each day acknowledging a few things that you love about yourself, and end each day telling yourself a few things that you appreciate about yourself from the day. Recognize all the different ways the people in your life show you love. Recognize all the different ways you express love to the people you care about in your life. Every time you are kind, smile at someone or at yourself, share compassion or understanding to someone making a mistake, judge someone for their kindness and beauty, and so on, you are being an expression of love. **We gain more fulfillment from the expression of love than we do from the receiving of love.** It is very important to receive, however, we accept love based on our internal belief of how much love we give. If you are acting like a bully, or not forgiving, or justifying negative behavior, you are not giving love, you are withdrawing it. Conversely, if you are caring, forgiving, and correcting negative behavior, you are being loving. This balances out your internal justice system to receive love for yourself.

The internal justice system is an often unspoken and subconscious balancing of the perception of our deeds. The following example is how I acted for a long time; actually until I decided to become a leader!

When you complain behind someone's back or to another person about another person, whether true, justified, or not, you will register that as a *negative inside yourself*. If the person you are complaining about is in a leadership role, for example, when an opportunity for you to take a leadership role arises, you will decline it and justify that decision by telling yourself you are not qualified. Very often this is because, below your level of awareness, you wouldn't step into a leadership role because you believe people would judge and complain about you – just like you did!

Our internal justice system maintains balance whether you are aware of it or not. So check here when you are not feeling loved.

THE NEED TO BELONG

When a person's need to belong is unfulfilled, like when they don't feel like they belong in a certain group or when they feel judged, they will become either the bully or victim. This is prevalent in schools, peer groups, work places, and even within the group dynamics of a home. The bully behavior emerges when there is internal judgment of a group and manifests itself as external taunting or putting down. The victim mindset emerges when a person begins complaining in a sad way about how the group is mean and unaccepting.

"If I get to be me, I belong. If I have to be like you, it's fitting in." This statement was told to author Brene' Brown by a twelve year-old! In many cases the person acting like a bully wants their victim to join them in their quest to fit in. The more the victim resists that quest, the more the bullying escalates. **Don't try to fit in.** Be who you truly want to be. Most of us are sending the message to ourselves and others that we need to fit in. But remember, fitting in will *never* feel like belonging.

I remember in seventh grade I wanted to be a part of the "popular" group of girls and boys. I was not, and I blamed it all on a couple of girls that I "knew" did not like me. I wasn't really sure if they liked me or not, but I made up all kinds of reasons why they didn't want me in the group. I spent most of my energy complaining rather than deciding to be myself and finding a group where I truly felt accepted. It is clear to me now that I simply was not focusing on being my magnificent self and picking the friends I wanted to hang out with. Instead, I was using a subjective, external standard to choose a friend group—the "popular" kids. No wonder I was having difficulty. In my seventh grade mind, that is where I thought I should *be* but not truly where I belonged.

Kids and people are not cruel or mean. Kids and people *act* mean, and this is not an indicator that they *are* mean. If you think about a time when you acted mean and you don't immediately attempt to justify the behavior, you will be able to see from tenderness that the way you acted was not the truth of who you know yourself to be. The way you acted was a result of something going on inside of you that was triggered from a circumstance or a situation outside of you. If this is true for you, it is true for everyone.

Fulfill the need to belong by inserting yourself into friend groups, family, organizations, etc., that you align with and with whom you'd like to spend time. Pour your love into people you love. Be interested in people; get to know them, and more importantly, let them get to know you.

I want to address the often-misunderstood group called cliques! It is important to know that cliques are a chosen family of friends. The challenges with cliques begin when you judge each other or compare. The way to avoid this is to be grateful for the chosen family of friends you are in, and notice other groups of cliques as chosen families of friends.

Another situation that causes you to feel like you don't belong is when you are trying to fit in or you are feeling like you don't fit in. Fitting in is the opposite of belonging. Fitting in is thinking or believing that you have to be like someone else in order to be accepted. Belonging wherever you are is when you are simply *being* your magnificent self. **When *being* your magnificent self, you belong wherever you are!**

An example of what I'm talking about occurred over and over for me with my siblings. I have six siblings, and we would connect with each other often through sarcasm and making fun of each other. I have a great ability to laugh at myself because of it, yet there came a time when I found I didn't like that anymore. I even began blaming them for my feeling of not belonging. I thought in order to be a part of the group and fit in, I had to be sarcastic, too. Once I realized that was not necessarily true, I did an experiment. I hung around them at family functions, like I always did, only I simply operated as myself. I chose to change the subject when they made fun of someone, or I said something kind. I admit that I also still sometimes chose to engage in sarcastic behavior. I did all of this without judging them or myself because that would not have been effective *or* a reflection of my magnificent self. When I operated this way, I knew I belonged because I had a feeling of genuineness that came with just speaking my truth.

THE NEED TO FEEL VALUABLE

The need to feel valuable is often unnoticed, and we don't do a very good job of paying attention to fulfilling this need for ourselves. We have over-identified our value with what we *do* rather than who we *are*. In other words, we are valuable because we were born and operate on this planet as a human being. **What we *do* gives us the opportunity to have an experience of our value.** By knowing this, it's less likely that I would want my value to be experienced as a bully or as a victim. I am sure you understand that the person acting like a bully is not being valuable at the moment they are acting like a bully. Conversely, the victim isn't being valuable at the moment they feel like a victim. Being valuable comes when you call upon your creativity. Creativity cannot be accessed when operating from force or resignation.

There is a difference between *feeling* valuable and being valuable. Feeling valuable comes and goes based on if you've learned to step back and let yourself experience your value. Being valuable is unshakeable.

Everyone deserves to experience being valuable. Fulfill the need to be valuable by taking time after each accomplishment to recognize the value it brings and in what ways.

An interesting way to recognize your value is to spend time with a baby. Notice how you feel about them, notice the joy they bring by *doing* nothing but *being* themselves. That is the truth of human beings. Our value is innate—we are valuable simply because we are born. **The way to *feel* our value is in our expression, in what we do.** Let me say this again. It isn't what you *do* that defines your value—you are already valuable. What you do gives you the *opportunity* to *feel* your value. So when you do something, acknowledge how you *feel* valuable.

THE NEED TO FEEL POWERFUL

The need to feel powerful is counteracted by *being* powerful and understanding the authentic description of power. A bully is operating from an unmet need to *be* powerful by overpowering. A victim is operating from an unmet need to be powerful by acting as if they have no power. Both ways are ineffective. Power is experienced from the inside out. **Power is used effectively, ineffectively, or misused.** For example, someone acting like a bully is misusing their power to hurt someone or to get their point across. A perceived victim is ineffective in that they are *not* using power. Imagine using your power to be valuable, to love, and to belong! This would be an effective use of power.

Using your power to be valuable is done when you shift from misusing power by bullying, to being valuable to the person instead. And you become valuable by recognizing and encouraging yourself to use *effective* power through words or actions.

There is an unshakeable and undeniable (powerful) inner strength that arises when you call upon your power to love and be loved. When people know they are loved no matter what, they have the strength (power) to be kind and compassionate. They have the strength to ask for what they want, and they have the strength to share the truth.

If you have the power to belong, you'll feel the inner power to express yourself authentically and genuinely, and you'll never question whether you belong or feel forced to fit in.

Fulfill the need to feel powerful by saying "yes" to the things that are important to you and when you are saying "no," know what you are saying "yes" to instead. For example, if I am saying "no" to going to a meeting, I say "no" while knowing I am actually saying "yes" to spending time with my kids instead. In addition to identifying what you want, continuously identify what's important to you and communicate that.

If we are talking about being powerful, then we must spend some time on the concept of powerlessness. When you are in a victim mindset, you will feel powerless, and when you are in a bully mindset you are simply an angry victim. *Feeling* powerless doesn't mean you *are* powerless. You feel powerless as a result of what you believe about yourself in that moment. You must interrupt this pattern by stopping and feeling the powerlessness and anger, then consciously deciding what you want. When you feel powerless, recognize that you may not be able to change the situation, but you can change the way you *feel* about yourself in the situation. This starts with a proactive approach of becoming familiar with your magnificent self and its expression.

Take the time to fulfill these basic needs for yourself first, and then you will be better able to identify if others are in need, and you can assist them.

Pam with her Dad – Forgiveness and love prevail.

I will listen to you.

I will not use anything you say against you.

I will respect you and your opinions.

I will not talk about you behind your back.

If I have an issue with you, I will discuss it directly with you.

If someone comes to me talking about you, I will direct them to you.

THE LEADERSHIP TRUST

Your Infinite Life Training & Coaching Company

CHAPTER 5

THE FEARS & BELIEFS

Now, back to setting a commitment. Fears may surface immediately after you've made a commitment, if you are awake enough to notice them! Learn how to recognize your fears from within, then face them intimately, rather than annihilating or running from them. This will be graceful through the process of discovering your beliefs.

Being afraid is part of life, and yet most of us were not taught how to face fear—we were generally taught to fight (bully) or run (victim). I say this because what occurs below your level of awareness is that as soon as fear comes anywhere close to your consciousness, you will either fight, freeze, or run from it. This shows up as arguing, defending, making excuses, avoidance, and denial, just to name a few!

In the bully/victim paradigm, we have become masters of avoiding fear by punishing the bully and arming the victim, yet this does not allow for facing the fear from the perspective of our magnificence, it only polarizes the dynamic and allows us to get further and further away from our magnificence.

Pema Chodron in her book, *When Things Fall Apart*, suggests we "*get to know fear, become familiar with fear, look it right in the eye—not as a way to solve problems, but as a complete undoing of old ways of seeing, hearing, smelling, tasting, and thinking.*" This is an amazing and humbling experience.

When one of my sons began to take the bus to first grade, he got off the bus every day crying. He was crying because there was a boy on the bus who was bullying him. Every day he cried, and every day I asked questions. "He calls me red-headed, freckle-face!" my son told me. I continued to ask questions. After every question I would say something that clearly implied he was the victim of this bully. He wanted me to drive him to school, and I said, "No, you must face that bully, and learn to deal with him because there will always be bullies in this world!" Well, the last day he was bullied arrived, and it came when I supported him while he faced that fear. As usual, he arrived from the bus crying. I asked him what was going on and he said, "Barry called me a red-headed, freckle-face." This was the point I decided it was time for him to face his fear, so I said, "Well, honey, you *are*!"

I knew this would alter his thinking, so I gave him a few seconds to register the comment. He looked at me puzzled and said, "What do you mean?" I said, "Well it is true that you have red hair and freckles, so why does it bother you that he keeps pointing that out?" He said, "Well, because he is saying it to make fun of me!" I said, "That may be true, so what do you want to do about *that*?" Notice I did not make an assumption (which would be arrogant) that this boy was intentionally being mean. I also gave him the problem back, by asking what he wanted to do. His answer was funny. He said, "I want to beat him up and tell him... (this is where he went on about all the mean things he wanted to say to him). At this point I explained that fighting back would not really solve the problem—it would be like me spanking him for hitting his brother. He understood it from this perspective. *(It's helpful to present this type of information without making them wrong, just offering another perspective.)* At that point he said he was not sure what to do except ignore him. We role played that scenario and he actually saw that it may be a hidden way to be mean because it would likely aggravate Barry. He could see this because I helped him see how upset he gets when someone ignores him. So, when I felt he was strong in his willingness to learn, I asked him if he wanted a suggestion. He did. I said, "Why don't you thank him for noticing? And say that without being mean, but by being truthful when you say thank you." He said, "Cool! I will do that tomorrow."

The next morning I reminded him of his plan and encouraged him. That afternoon he got off the bus with the biggest smile I had ever seen! I asked how it went. He explained that the scenario was the same, with Barry calling him red-headed, freckle-face, and he simply said, "thank you for noticing." It must have caught Barry off-guard because he laughed and was quiet for the rest of the ride. He was never bullied after that because he was never afraid of being bullied because he discovered that he can be magnificent when he faces his fears. In this specific case, the fear was that there was something bad about him because he had red hair and freckles. Facing this fear completely undid his old way of thinking, seeing, and hearing about his belief about himself.

Most of us have never been told to stop running from our fear, so we do what comes naturally, which is to check out or freak out. The way to shift the paradigm is to hang in there and keep exploring. With practice, my son came to know his own courage, strength, compassion and so much more. **Brave people have not conquered fear, nor do they never feel afraid—brave people are intimate with fear.**

To become intimate with fear, and to diminish a fear, develop trust in your ability to handle anything. This will require a shift in some beliefs and expectations. Most of our fears, especially in relationships with others are the result of beliefs and expectations formed during experiences at a very young age. In the example of the bus ride with Barry, you can see that John had beliefs and expectations that limited him in believing in his magnificence and his abilities to trust himself to handle that differently. Look at this perspective from the drawing:

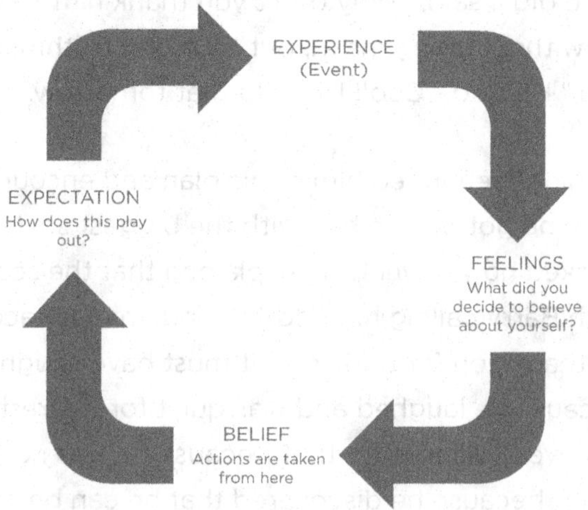

An event occurs. We have feelings, and from these feelings we decide what to believe about ourselves, life, men, women and what to do. The belief is solidified through the action we choose to take. The action driven from the belief creates the expectation. Maintaining that expectation will cause future experiences that *feel* the same.

FOR EXAMPLE:
Experience (Event) – John rides the bus home from school and during the ride Barry makes fun of him, calling him a "red-headed, freckle-face."

Feelings and Decisions – He felt scared and hurt. He decided that having red hair and freckles was a bad thing. Also decided that boys bigger than him are potential bullies.

Belief and Actions – I am powerless around bigger boys because I have red hair and freckles. I should be afraid. The action was withdrawal and acting afraid around Barry, as well as giving dirty looks to accentuate the fear of him.

Expectation – He expected Barry to treat him the same every time. He expected to be afraid, have a terrible bus ride, and be made fun of every day. This expectation occurred despite thinking it would be different.

You can see that as soon as we formulate a belief, in this case a limiting belief, we do things below our level of awareness that perpetuate the belief. We actually unconsciously begin to trust in the limiting belief. From our expectation we invalidate our trust in ourselves and others, and continue to freeze, run from, or fight with the fear. So the key to change is to first become aware of the limiting belief, change the belief, and take new actions based on the new belief, thereby creating new expectations. Every time you take a new action based from a new, expanded belief, you develop more trust in yourself as magnificent—as someone who is greater than the one who is currently falling victim to a limited way of thinking.

Pushing away an old or limiting belief does not eliminate it. Take the time to walk through the process for yourself. Think of an experience or event that did not turn out the way you wanted.

> There is an experience or an event.
>
> This experience causes a feeling or feelings. **Discover what those feelings are. It is important to focus on some aspect of the following feelings - mad, sad, afraid, hurt, or happy.** Once the feelings are identified, ask yourself: **"Based on this feeling, what did I decide to believe about myself, life or men or women or authorities?"**
>
> The answer to this question is the belief. This will help you see that your actions after the belief was formed came from the limits you placed on yourself. This will also give you insight into your expectations.
>
> To discover more about your current expectations, ask the question: **"How is this limiting belief playing out currently in my life?"**
>
> Now to develop a new way, decide on a new belief for yourself. To identify how to move beyond, ask yourself the question: **What is my new belief about myself? or What would I have needed to believe about myself in order to respond or feel differently?**
>
> The next step is to develop a new action and anchor that action. **Take a couple of action steps to anchor the new belief within the next three days.**
>
> This new action will create a new expectation.

When feeling like the victim, it's critical to access and understand the feeling and pain you are in, however you must be connected to the possibility of the magnificent self and, guide yourself from that perspective so you don't stay a victim or a bully.

Ask yourself once again, "Am I willing to commit to not harming others or myself with my words or actions?" Then ask, "Am I willing to be responsible for that commitment?" Keep in mind that you will now have the opportunity to be conscious of any limiting beliefs or doubts you have about your new-found commitment. It will be an opportunity to become intimate with those fears, and go on the journey of discovery using the tool above.

People grow up believing that responsibility means meeting other people's expectations and avoiding messing up. Rather, responsibility is your behavior, but more importantly, *your* attitudes. You have an effect on each and every person you deal with, whether by text, phone, social media, e-mail, paper, or in person. If it comes from your voice, expression, body language, or writing, you affect them. Paying attention to that interaction is being responsible for it.

Using this tool or process is an opportunity to work *through* something rather than *on* something. You will feel more empowered and be more productive in your responsibility for your magnificence. One way to know you are in your magnificence is when you are truly aligned mentally, emotionally, physically, and spiritually. If you feel something but don't understand it, or understand something but don't feel it, this is the point at which seeking to discover a limiting belief will help you along the path of being increasingly responsible for your innate magnificence.

Boys into Men – Celebrating!

“Our deepest fear is not that we are inadequate.
Our deepest fear is that we are powerful beyond measure.
It is our light, not our darkness,
that most frightens us.
We ask ourselves, who am I to be brilliant,
gorgeous, talented, and fabulous?
Actually, who are we not to be?
You are a child of God.
Your playing small does not serve the world.
There’s nothing enlightened about shrinking so that
other people won’t feel insecure around you.
You were born to make manifest
the glory of God that is within you.
It’s not just in some of us, it’s in everyone.
And as we let our own light shine, we unconsciously
give other people permission to do the same.
As we are liberated from our own fears,
Our presence automatically liberates others.”

MARIANNE WILLIAMSON

CHAPTER 6

STEP ASIDE – OBSERVE – CHANGE

Once fears are understood intimately, we can see the limits of the bully and victim inside ourselves. Then, by asking yourself the right questions, you will be able to self-reliantly expand into the expression of magnificence that will allow you to reach beyond all previous understandings.

We are all from time to time the casualties and cause of emotional damage. In other words, we have all been the victim, the bully, and the bystander. You may not have bullied the way someone you judge harshly has bullied. You may not have been a victim to the extent of the victim you feel the most pity for. You may have many reasons why it was important for you to be the bystander.

It is painful to face how we harm others and ourselves when acting like a bully, a bystander, or a victim. There is no justification *and* there is no judgment for when you do. Remember, no judgment is the act of suspending your judgment of a person—separating the deed from the doer. No judgment along with no justification equals compassion.

NO JUDGMENT + NO JUSTIFICATION = COMPASSION
NO JUDGMENT + NO JUSTIFICATION = FREEDOM OF RESPONSIBILITY

Another one of those great ideas, right? Impossible, you say? I say, *no way*! This may not be something you can accomplish in your lifetime, however, it can be something you strive for because in doing so, you will serve your magnificence as well as the magnificence of others.

This is a great time to stop talking to yourself, get curious, and start listening instead. Listen to what you are *really* saying. Listen to what themes occupy your thoughts. What are your fears, concerns, worries, limiting beliefs, judgments? At first the silence (remember the Silent Space) expands into our fear, resentments, pain, anger, the beliefs about who we think we are, and who we think they are. This silence will bring forth what is residing in our subconscious—what you are unaware of currently. From this point, you can learn to tame your negativity, fears, resentments, and pain with compassion.

Let me share a story that will explain what I am talking about. Sharon and Henry have a solid marriage. They are blessed with one daughter, Anna, whom they love dearly. Life seemed to be moving along smoothly. Anna was about ten years old when they decided to move to a larger home. Sharon and Henry had no idea that this move would cause stress because they were so excited. However, the move caused a considerable amount of stress. Henry had to spend a significant amount of time preparing to sell the old house, while Sharon and Anna were making the new house a home. This meant that Henry was not around a lot for a few months. Sharon and Henry's personal struggles with the move triggered a significant behavior change in Anna. She became angry and depressed and frequently threatened. The behavior resulted in her yelling a lot and being physically abusive mainly toward Sharon. Sharon's response to this behavior was to either curl into a ball on the floor (victim) or be aggressive toward Anna (bully). Moving through this process to bring harmony back into the house was a process that required much soul-searching, listening to themselves and each other, as well as using tools from many resources.

First, everyone in the family had to acknowledge their desire to have things different. Then they had to make a commitment to change. Anna had to be inspired to change as well. There was curiosity to be discovered, limiting beliefs to move beyond, habitual responses to change, and healing to be done. Each month brought gradual improvement as its reward. Sharon remembers that while she had told Anna many times that her (Anna's) behavior was unacceptable, it wasn't until she (Sharon) believed in herself and made her bully behavior unacceptable that things began to change. Much work had to be done by all three of them to raise their individual levels of self-esteem by discovering, honoring and then expressing their magnificence.

If you choose your level of commitment, rather than it choosing you, and you operate from an unlimited belief, you will be better equipped to ride the middle of the road where there are no victims and no bullies. You will be able to see that others may be acting like a bully and/or acting like a victim, yet you know it is only an act, not truly who they are.

BEING YOUR OWN AUTHORITY

Riding the middle of road becomes easier when you can be more conscious of being your own authority. Let me explain.

An **authority** is a person with extensive or specialized knowledge about a subject - an expert. Authorities pose no threat; in fact, they have the potential to be of great value. We may take advantage of their expertise to improve our lives and to achieve our goals. For example, when an automobile is not running well we may take it to a mechanic (an authority on the functioning of automobiles) for a diagnoses and, possibly, corrective action. There are many authorities in our lives, and you are an authority of certain things as well. The key to taking full advantage of the authority's expertise is to remember that no matter what they say, the responsibility for deciding on what action to take as well as taking responsibility for that action always remains with us.

An **authority figure** is someone (or something) that from our viewpoint holds the responsibility for and the consequences of our actions and decisions. When the leaders we make authority figures challenge us or hold us accountable, we often act uncooperatively in an effort to resist what we think they may be forcing us to do. Additionally, we may further avoid responsibility by blaming our uncooperative behavior on the authority figures, who in our lives show up as parents, teachers, bosses, therapists, coaches. When we create the feeling that someone else is our authority figure, we often forget to act on our own initiative and in alignment with our personal, moral, and ethical beliefs (our conscience). The consequence of creating authority figures is a failure to hold ourselves accountable and responsible for the results of our decisions and actions. A symptom of creating authority figures is when you are blaming.

We are our own authority in that we are fully accountable for all of the consequences of our decisions and actions. We are our own authority in that we choose how we express ourselves through what we do, how we feel about what we do, and how we feel about what others do.

Being your own authority translates into being fully accountable to all of the consequences of your decisions and actions—the perceived bad and good. Being your own authority means that you behave and express yourself with the attitude of "everything I do, think, and feel in every moment of my life is my choice." Even when it seems that what is happening in a given situation is beyond your control, you still have the ability to choose how you will respond to the situation.

So, you can see that being your own authority means that you can ride the middle of the road because you won't be a bully or a victim, and you certainly wouldn't see others as bullies or victims. Relationships work best when viewed as a circle as opposed to a straight line. In the circle, there is no first, no last, no better, no worse—and in that circle, everyone present has a contribution, no matter what it looks like because there is purpose for everyone in the circle and the sense of ordering goes away.

In the story about Henry, Sharon, and Anna, you can see how each of them began by making one another the authority figure.

At some point, there will be rebellion in a relationship where one person has made another their authority figure. When Sharon was struggling with Anna's behavior and either curling into a ball or being aggressive, she had made Anna the authority figure. When Anna was being aggressive and threatening, she was making her parents authority figures (she viewed them as the cause of her unhappiness). Through the healing and learning process, they moved into being their own authority. This let them stand on their own, centered and anchored in their own magnificent expression.

POWERFUL QUESTIONS - CAN I SHIFT MY MINDSET BY SIMPLY ASKING THE RIGHT QUESTIONS?

A powerful question, or line of questioning, is designed to lead the person you are asking toward their magnificence, toward accountability, and away from victim mindset and/or justifying bully behavior. Powerful questions can assist you in becoming your own authority as well. But there is such a thing as a "circular" question. A circular question is one that leads your mind, and your life for that matter, into a loop. Circular questions lead you to feeling like you are moving through quicksand - trying to get somewhere, yet sinking further and further. Circular questions are self-depreciating, self-defeating, or ignite negative feelings about others, such as: "Why are kids so cruel or mean? Why would you act that way? Why did you do that? Why do you feel that way about what happened? Why do you think he is picking on you?" As you can see, a circular question often begins with "why." Asking why will keep you in the loop of where you are and spiraling down further into the same situation.

To make the best use of a question, you need to un-learn many of your current question-behaviors and attitudes. You may need to exercise some self-discipline through asking yourself powerful questions.

> Most questions begin with: how, what, where, who, and why.
>
> Ineffective or circular questions often start with either a why... or a what if...
>
> Why can't I look like that?
>
> What if she doesn't stop being mean to me?
>
> Why did he do that to me?
>
> What if I'm not good enough?
>
> Why can't things be different?
>
> Why did this happen to me?
>
> What if she's just that way?
>
> Why doesn't he like me?

This type of thinking encourages intellectualization and often results in speculation, fabrication, and presumption. Wondering what others are thinking or doing, for that matter, is a complete waste of time. Refocus your energy. Take the time spent worrying and reinvest it in yourself. Your imagination will help you.

To develop quality questions, use examples such as:

> How...? How can...? How can I...?
>
> What can I do to...? What needs to happen to...?

Where can...? Where can I...? Where can I find...?

When can...? When can I...? When can I have...?

"Why can't I look like that?" becomes: "How do I want to look?" "What can I do to look like that?" "When can I look like that?"

"What if she won't stop being mean to me?" becomes: "How can I have her behavior not affect me?" "What do I need to believe about myself in order to feel better?" "Where can I find the support I need?"

Self-reliant thinking is the opposite of a victim mindset. Here is a chart that will demonstrate the difference and give you a point of reference.

BEING YOUR OWN AUTHORITY

Self-Reliant Mindset	Victim Mindset
Heart focused with the balance of the mind: constantly heading in the direction toward what you want.	Result only focused. Constantly wanting to be better or higher to prove how good you are. Looking for your own superiority, or validating the victim.
In what way is this in my best interest? In what way is this not in my best interest?	Will this lead to success or failure? How can I keep my inadequacies from becoming apparent?
Is doing this the best way I can be of service to magnificence?	What are they going to demand from me?
If I decide to do this, is there a way I can leverage my service/helpfulness?	How can I do as little as possible and still have what I want?
Do I have the energy to do this? If I don't have the energy, in what way can I increase my energy?	This is going to take too much time or too much of myself.
Do I have the money to do this? If I do not have the money, in what way can I be creative in order to do what I want?	That is too much money or that is a lot of money! I don't want to have to work harder or more to pay for it. I am doing all I can now.
I know there will be both benefits and challenges if I do this. Some of the benefits and challenges can be anticipated, and some of them will be unexpected. Am I willing to handle whatever comes up?	How can I postpone this decision? How long can I procrastinate doing what I say I want to do?
In what way will doing what is asked of me inspire the people for whom I would be doing this?	I must not let them talk me into anything.
What is the value to me? And if I do not go for getting the value here, where else will I get it?	The victim mindset does not take time to look to see value, so I would not realize that I'm missing anything.
Inquires and investigates to see the benefits and if there are none, no offense is taken.	Addresses the interaction in a way that makes me feel the authority figure is trying to make me do something.
Is always looking for a way to say yes, to make the other right.	Makes being right more important than being close.
Know I can be happy in any situation. Know that the way I feel is a decision, my decision.	Let the circumstances and the drama determine how I feel.
I am spiritually, mentally, emotionally and physically taking care of myself in order to be who I want to be.	I blame others or situations for my feelings of tiredness, lack of inspiration or motivation, or illness.
Am I living from my purpose?	Am I living up to other people's expectations?

Honor, commitment and courage from all.

"Feelings are meant to be felt, not necessarily expressed."

PAMELA DUNN

CHAPTER 7

THE DEEPER MEANING OF FEELINGS & TONE

Deepening your understanding of feelings and tone allows for heightened intuition, greater compassion, and an increased faith in your own ability. Feelings are a key component to conflict resolution. Tone is a verbal expression of feelings that already exist within.

I AM – I FEEL – I THINK!

People respond to how they *feel* about what you say more than the words you use. Often in our communication with others, we focus on or worry about the words we use. While using effective language is helpful, it is equally important to be consciously aware of *your* feelings in your communication. This next resource will help you integrate your language with your feelings to produce effective communication without needlessly labeling yourself into a limiting belief, which occurs when you use "I am" in front of a word.

Say to yourself, "I am tired." Now say, "I feel tired." Say to yourself, "I am annoyed." Now say, "I feel annoyed." Whatever you say after the words, "I am" has you making a statement that infers your *way of being* (a belief) and who you are. **Who you are is so much more than tired, annoyed, mad, sad, happy, and so on.** It's true that you feel all of these feelings sometimes, however it is not an indication of who you are; you simply feel or think that way in that present moment.

The key to being in charge of yourself and your feelings is to feel your feelings and identify them rather than over-identifying with your feelings as being who you are. Over-identification occurs when you say "I am (insert whatever feeling you have)."

Once you identify what you are *feeling*, before you respond, take time to *feel* the feeling. This is how it's done: ***Recognize where in your body the feeling originates. > Put your hand on that place on your body. > With your intention, follow the feeling down through your feet and up through the top of your head. > Once this is complete – THEN RESPOND.***

The more you practice with "I feel..." the more comfortable you will become with any and all feelings. You will give yourself permission to recognize the perceived negative feelings because you will know **you are simply feeling the feeling, *you* are not the feeling**.

Because we grow up hearing and using language like, "I am mad at you" or "you are making me so angry," we actually begin to deny those feelings and/or blame others for our feelings. It is understood that if *I feel* a certain way, I can *feel* another way when I choose. Yes, it is true you can and do choose your feelings! This is generated through your thoughts. So if you want to understand how you came about feeling a certain way, begin by discovering what you are thinking. Here is a resource for that process.

I realize that it doesn't always seem like we choose our feelings. **The way to become more conscious and better understand the feelings you are choosing is to pay attention to and recognize your tone of voice.** Your tone of voice (what is expressed on the outside) is an indication of what you are feeling on the inside and begins to tell the story of what you were thinking about yourself (or men, or women, or life, or the situation, etc.) that brought on that feeling.

Tone is the verbal expression of a feeling. Our tone and feelings help us know if we are aligned with our stated values, beliefs, intentions, or goals. You see, we do not always *behave* based on those stated values, beliefs, intentions, or goals. We often *behave* based on what we feel, whether conscious or not! Sometimes our tone (the verbal expression of our feelings) derails our best efforts. This is actually done below our level of awareness. I'll give you an example: I was on a hike with my sons. Tom had a very long stick he was pretending was a spear. He was aiming it at certain things ahead of us and throwing it, then running ahead to pick it up. He had been doing this for quite a while when he aimed at something, threw the "spear" and missed his stated target. Without hesitation he ran ahead, picked up the "spear" and threw it in the woods, yelling "stupid spear!" I laughed out loud! I asked him, "Do you really think it's the spear's fault for missing your target?" He didn't really understand my question because how could it be the spear's fault! So I explained that he was the one throwing the spear and guiding the spear, so perhaps he was the one responsible for it not reaching the target. But because he was judging himself for not reaching the target, he used a tone (anger) and words that suggested it was the spear's fault. When doing *this*, he does not have to assume any responsibility for becoming a better aim.

This may seem like a silly example and appear difficult to translate to relationships, but it is quite typical of what we do regularly with people. For example, once while traveling, I arrived at the airport later than I had originally planned. I was waiting in the security line internally huffing, puffing, and rolling my eyes because the people in front of me were taking so long! You see, if I had arrived on time, I wouldn't need to be worried about time. However, since I was the one who was late, my huffing, puffing, and rolling of eyes gave me the *feeling* that if I missed my flight it would be the fault of the people in front of me, *not* me—even though intellectually (my stated belief) I would tell you it was my fault I was late!

This story shows us so many things: like the subtle ways we blame (huffing, rolling of the eyes, throwing things, etc.), or the automatic, yet somewhat ridiculous idea that blaming someone else for being late is effective. If you had asked me right after that if I thought it was someone else's fault that I was late, I would have definitely said, "No!" It is simply funny to recognize how we unconsciously blame through the use of our tone (the feelings inside that already exist). **Pay attention to this! A habit of blaming leads to bullying behavior, feeling like a victim and strips you of the chance to learn through taking responsibility for your own actions.** This is why it's essential to take a look at our tone, or *the verbal expression of our feelings on the inside*, to assess if those are the feelings we wish to communicate, and if they aren't, find another way to consciously respond.

This was previously stated, yet bears repeating here. Once you identify what you are feeling, before you respond, you will want to feel the feeling. The way to do that is – ***recognize where in your body the feeling originates > put your hand on that place on your body > then follow the feeling down through your feet and up through the top of your head > once this is complete – then respond.***

Until we completely feel the feeling throughout ourselves, we will likely project the feeling. In other words, we will, for example feel angry, then proceed to tell the person that triggered this feeling that we are angry with them for their behavior. This has the potential of causing unnecessary conflict because you will be inadvertently blaming them for your angry feelings. If you fully feel the feeling, you will respond from a place of compassion *and* a matching tone. This will help you get more of what you want from the relationship. This process works better than explaining why someone "made" you feel angry.

VARIOUS TONES AND TURN AROUNDS

Tone & Feeling	Thoughts	Insights, Turn Arounds, and Questions
Angry Disappointed	"I can't get them to do what I want." "I am a bad manager/leader/ parent etc." "Why can't they do or say what I want them to?"	Realize we use anger to disguise the feeling of powerlessness. You can actually feel powerful at the exact time you are claiming that others have power. Realize you feel powerless. Discover for yourself three ways to get what you want. What is it that you can do to change this situation?
Disgusted Complaining	"If only others were more capable, I would not be experiencing this difficulty." "I've done all I can."	Realize we use disgust to feel superior without having to take action or switch to compassion. Do something valuable or helpful for the person you have decided to be disgusted with. What can you do to improve this situation, even if it is to improve your perspective?
Irritated Annoyed	"My lack of serenity is caused by circumstances or the behavior of others." "If only ..."	Realize we use feelings of irritation to justify putting the responsibility of the situation outside ourselves. Do what you want in the moment while telling yourself 3 things you appreciate about yourself. Practice serenity. What is it that you really want or need?
Frustrated	"Things outside my control block me." "It is not working" "I've tried everything!"	Realize we use frustration to justify quitting prior to giving full effort. Re-commit to what you want and take one more step towards that goal with an action. What is one thing you can do to move forward?
Rushed	"I am too busy to do all this." "I should be doing something else but...."	Realize we use "rushed" to make us feel important often in moments when we are unsure of ourselves. Relax. Remind yourself that what you do is not who you are. Contribute by acting purposefully rather than urgently. What do you think is the most important thing you could do right now? How can I help you?

Tone & Feeling	Thoughts	Insights, Turn Arounds, and Questions
Indecisive Risk Adverse	"If I commit, they will hold me accountable." "I didn't have enough information to wisely decide." "What if it's the wrong decision?" "What if...?"	Realize we use indecisiveness because we are afraid to make mistakes, and want to justify avoiding accountability. Make a decision and then make it the best decision through your actions. Does it really matter what you choose? Why?
Dissatisfaction	"Because of them (their inability...) I am not getting what I need or expected." "He/she is not meeting my needs."	Realize that we use dissatisfaction to justify leaning on others to improve the situation. Do for yourself what you are dissatisfied about. What is it that you actually expected? What is it that you really want?
Guilt	"I've done something I wish I would not have done" "It's all my fault." "I should have ..." "I should not have ..."	Realize we use guilt to feel we have made amends without having to do anything to make up for what we feel guilty about. If you feel guilty, you are guilty. Do a make-up for the person you have been inconsiderate to. Is there anything you would have done differently in this situation?
Hurt	"I feel hurt that you did not reward my effort in an appropriate way" "You should have...." "Why does it/them have to be that way?"	Realize we thought we were doing something for somebody else, but actually we were doing it for our own recognition; your actions had a "hook. You were fishing rather than feeding the fish. Ask for what you really want and be responsible for getting it. How did it feel?
Stressed	"I have so much to do I don't know where to start." Am I capable of doing everything?"	Realize we are overwhelming ourselves to avoid setting priorities and taking responsibility. How did it get to this point? What is my purpose?

ANOTHER OVER-IDENTIFICATION TRAP!

Just like saying "I am (insert feeling here)" creates an over-identification with the feeling by leading us to believe we are that feeling rather than we simply have a feeling, using the word "my" can also develop over-identification and attachment.

There are two really great ways to explain this. Think about the toddler that grabs the toy someone else has and says, "*mine*!" This may sound trivial, however we learn to claim possession then. That possession comes through in our adult years as *my* son, daughter, friend, car, house, and so on. Let me be clear; I realize that is true. In other words, when we say "my ..." it is true, yet pay attention to your tone and if you are putting extra emphasis on the word, "my," because it will tell you if you are over-identifying with what follows that word.

Freedom exists when you learn that nothing *really* belongs to you; you are simply the steward of everything you encounter. Surrender to your desires, and let go of everything in the way of those desires. Very often when we hear that we would benefit from letting go, we automatically make the assumption we have to let go of people. This is very often not the case. Most of the time if you let go of the limiting beliefs that no longer serve your desires or magnificence, that usually proves to be enough. To explain this further, let me share a story about a friend I assisted.

My friend Lucy was challenged in her relationship with her parents. Lucy was twenty-four years old, lived with her boyfriend in a different city than her parents, and had a great full-time job. She was challenged in this new city because she hadn't made friends and was working from home. Before she realized it, she was unhappy and nearly miserable. Every time she spoke with her parents, she shared her feelings and her misery.

One evening, "out of the blue," her parents called her to tell her she needed to get a grip on her health and get on medication. Lucy felt completely blindsided and misunderstood. I began asking some questions. We quickly discovered that she was operating from a subconscious, limiting belief that her parents were the ones that were responsible for creating her happiness. This just happened to be something she decided without realizing it at a very young age.

Once she saw this consciously, she could see where she was validating that belief. It explained for her a lot of her dissatisfaction.

She graciously explained to her parents how she was now going to take over the responsibility for her happiness and thanked them for how supportive they always are. This shift sent the message to herself that she had to turn on her creativity to make her own happiness. Just knowing the limiting belief helped her take a different action.

CONFLICT RESOLUTION

Any conflict or any situation you want to address needs to be addressed inside of you first and must be looked at mentally, emotionally, physically and spiritually. If you are conflicted about a person or situation, it's important to come to peace inside yourself before addressing it with anyone, especially the person or people involved in the conflict. We are generally taught to avoid conflict or to address conflict head on. Neither one of these approaches creates the peace we desire. The peace we desire actually is the peace within. We think that peace within will come when we handle the conflict with the other person. That may not be true. I have a different approach: Don't avoid the conflict! Instead, ask yourself these questions: "What does this feeling say about me?" "What story is the feeling telling me?" "What do I think this conflict is saying about me?" Reconcile any limiting beliefs you may have about yourself, life, or others as a result of the conflict. Once this is complete, there will be a good way to communicate as you go about resolving the conflict (which now may not seem so much like a conflict, but a way to get what you want).

COMMUNICATION MODEL FOR CONFLICT RESOLUTION AND A GOOD WAY TO ASK FOR WHAT YOU WANT

PICK THE RIGHT MOMENT

Ask if it is an okay time to talk about something that is important to you. If you are told "no," ask when would be a good time. People can hear you better if you approach them at a time when they are not preoccupied or stressed.

CHOOSE THE RIGHT WORDS

Be genuine in the sharing of your feelings. In other words, feel your feelings as you share them, without the need to blame the other person for how you feel. Remember, how you feel is for and about you. No one can "make you feel" a certain way. This is an opportunity to help the other person understand what is important to you. Start your communication with:

- ***I Feel*** ... *Example* - I feel annoyed
- **When** ... *Example* - When I call and leave a message, my call is never returned.

Avoid “you” as this creates defensiveness when what you want is resolution.

OWN YOUR PART IN THE CONFLICT

This is a great time to examine, acknowledge to yourself, and share how things affect you. For example, sometimes our part is that we withhold what is important to us because we believe it wouldn’t be valued. So you are deciding to act differently in the future when you share your part. Again, be sure to communicate without blaming, and perhaps use language like:

> ***My part is*** ... *Example* – I have never communicated that calling me back is important.

ARTICULATE SPECIFICALLY WHAT YOU WANT

State directly and clearly what you want (not what you don’t want). Develop action plans that accommodate everyone by staying curious about what you want and inquiring about what they want. Together you can come up with something that works for everyone.

> **What I want is** ... *Example* – for you to call me back within twenty-four hours.

> **Will you? This is a crucial question!**

COMMIT TO ACTION AND COMMUNICATE YOUR COMMITMENT

This will be necessary when you want more freedom or responsibility. Share what you can be counted on to do and also be willing to be held accountable. Start your commitment statements with:

> **You can count on me to ...**

INCLUDE OTHERS IN THE PLAN

In some cases, you will want to be curious about what they want as well. This way of caring shows that you are truly committed to an action plan that works for everyone. This is the place where you will want to make sure you stay curious, and monitor your limiting beliefs in case you have a challenge with anything that is stated.

> ***Is there anything that you need in order to give me what I want?***

MIRROR, MIRROR, MIRROR.

> **What I heard you say was ...**

This is vital in the communication process. You will want to do lots of mirroring because it helps you gain a deeper understanding and clarification of what is being said. Don't worry about getting it wrong or about them getting it wrong. This is the opportunity to be sure that they feel heard. So if the mirror is off, simply let them know what they missed. You can even ask, "Did I get that right?" "What did I miss?"

In some challenging conversations interrupting becomes a problem. If this becomes a problem, tell the person that's interrupting you that what you are talking about is important to you and ask them if they would be willing to wait until you are finished before they speak. Promise them that you will listen intently to them when you are finished. If this doesn't work, you may want to listen to them first. It is sometimes easier for people to listen after they have been heard. While listening to them, teach them how you want them to treat you by not defending and only mirroring back to them.

If you are asking for something you want, it's crucial to always end by saying:

> **Will you?**

Nature guides and shows truth.

"People are often unreasonable, illogical, and self-centered.
FORGIVE THEM ANYWAY.
If you are kind, people may accuse you of selfish, ulterior motives.
BE KIND ANYWAY.
If you are successful, you will win some false friends and some true enemies.
SUCCEED ANYWAY.
If you are honest and frank, people may cheat you.
BE HONEST AND FRANK ANYWAY.
What you spend years building, someone could destroy overnight.
BUILD ANYWAY.
If you find serenity and happiness, they may be jealous.
BE HAPPY ANYWAY.
The good you do today, people will often forget tomorrow.
DO GOOD ANYWAY.
Give the world the best you have, and it may never be enough.
GIVE THE WORLD THE BEST YOU HAVE ANYWAY.
You see in the final analysis, it is between you and God.
IT WAS NEVER BETWEEN YOU AND THEM ANYWAY."

MOTHER TERESA

CHAPTER 8

CHARACTER TRAITS & CONCEPTS TO MASTER

Here are several more character traits and concepts that you'll want to develop and master in order to eliminate the bully/victim paradigm, and begin to see yourself and everyone through the lens of magnificence.

PERSONAL WILL/WILL POWER/ DIVINE (MAGNIFICENCE) WILL

"If I treat you as though you ARE what you are capable of becoming, I help you become that."
Goethe

Personal will is when you decide you want to be or behave a certain way. We can definitely will ourselves to behave a certain way, in other words, from our magnificence. Yet, we all know that at the moment that becomes difficult, our personal will is ineffective. Your magnificence will always be something way beyond anything you were taught. This is because it is *your* magnificence and must be discovered and uncovered.

Personal will is developed and operates from your current belief system, therefore is limited and ever-evolving based on your ability to understand and develop it. So, when you attempt to take yourself beyond your current abilities, your personal will becomes ineffective, and you need to call upon your willpower. We use willpower in many ways, such as demanding, pushing and saying things like, "get over it, and do it anyway!" There is a more graceful approach which is by calling upon your Divine Will. Divine Will turns a demand into a preference and a push into a graceful forward movement. Grace doesn't mean it's not difficult or challenging. Grace means there is forward movement.

Example: I have the intention to be encouraging to my children. One of them comes home with a D on a test. At that moment I am inclined to demand and force them to study more and harder; telling them what they need to do. As we all know, this method is generally ineffective and invites bullying behavior, which means your child will feel like a victim. The way out of this paradigm is to call upon Divine Will. This is done by first remembering that your child is magnificent and this happens to be a place where that magnificence is not reflected.

Here are some questions that you can use to shift you and others from personal will/will power to the grace of Divine Will:

How do you feel about your result?

Would you like a different result? What is your preference?
What benefits would be gained from the different result?
How would that feel?

Imagine yourself accomplishing that result!

Let's brainstorm some ideas on what is needed in order to accomplish this result. What do you think you need?

What is the first step you will take to move in the direction of the result you prefer to accomplish?

If the answers are that they don't care or they are content with the result, then it will be important to discover what has caused them to stop caring.

DETACHMENT AND SURRENDER

"He who would be serene and pure needs but one thing, detachment."
Meister Ekhart

"If you want anything, you must detach." I've said this, and I've heard many others say this, but what does it mean? I know that if I am attached, I will be controlling, demanding, anxious, pressuring, and so on. Then if I am unattached, I will be in a state of pretending

I don't care, or in denial, or assuming the "Universe" will handle everything! So it seems obvious that detached is somewhere in between. Detached is patient, peaceful, and trusting. Detachment simply means "without fear." So therefore, detachment is full of love. How do you detach from what you want? How do you detach from difficult situations *and* go for what you want? Detachment equals an open heart. This means that in order to detach, you must surrender. Let me be clear that when I say "surrender," I do *not* mean to give in. I mean to surrender to what you want, surrender to the love you have for the outcome you desire, release your fears, open your heart, and begin the journey to your desire.

Here is a story that illustrates the kind of surrender I'm talking about. My son was home on leave for a total of thirty days. When that leave was over, he would be moving to Japan for what we all thought was three years. As you can imagine, I had the intention of taking advantage of every moment possible to spend time with him. I could tell that I was very excited about being with him, and there also was a hint of desperation about making sure I spent "enough" time with him. In reflection, I wonder what constitutes, "enough" when you are preparing for your son to leave for three years! So at the beginning of his leave, I was relaxed and was satisfied with ten minutes or ten hours with him. At about two weeks into his leave and with about two weeks left, I began measuring how much time he was spending with me. I was focused on the amount of time and instantly lost sight of the actual time I was with him as well as the enjoyment of being with him. I was attached to spending time with him, and because I was not detached, I was afraid I would not have "enough" time with him. At the moment I became aware of my desperation and fears, I simply focused on how much I love my son. Right after that came the tears! I realized I had become attached when I got afraid of the feelings I had about his leaving, about how our relationship would change, how my role as a mother was about to change again. The moment I detached, I felt all those feelings (for about fifteen minutes) and then I was relaxed, detached and full of the expression of love I know as myself from my magnificence.

It is important to be prepared to surrender to your desire and detach from the way you accomplish that desire. There was no way I could ever have had enough time with my son, but I could spend the time I had with him focused on the love we share.

Here are some questions you can ask yourself to move from fear to detachment, as well as to identify what you need to surrender to:

> What am I feeling? If I am feeling anything other than inner peace and love, then go to the next question.
>
> What is it that I really want?
>
> Have I surrendered to my desire? If not, do so.
>
> What or whom do I love? What shall I pour my love into?
>
> What shall I do now?

LETTING GO

"There is enough for everyone's need, but not for everyone's greed."
Gandhi

Letting go is often associated with surrender, however there is a difference. Surrender is about surrendering to your desire, to your destiny. Surrender is a spiritual concept. Letting go is the key to accomplishing that desire or destiny because you must let go of everything in the way of that accomplishment (what you have surrendered to).

It is the wise individual who can graciously let go. Letting go is easier when you stay away from the over-identification trap described in Chapter Seven. There may be a time when you must let go of things, but **letting go of your attitude about something is the most important focus.** When you first let go of your attitude, you are better able to know and let go of anything else that does not serve you, your magnificence, and your desires.

Let go of your idea of what you think everything should look like. *Be* present to how things *are*. For example, if you have been or know someone who is being bullied, there will be a tendency to focus on how things should be and how no one should be subjected to this bullying. It is truly the moment in which you will want to lean into the feelings that are occurring for you. Once you *feel* the feelings, you can let them go. This is the moment when you can respond from your magnificence. Letting go allows you to eliminate the bully/victim paradigm, to see each person as a person, rather than a label; this is the freedom of no justifications + no judgment = responsibility.

We fight letting go, and most of the time we hold onto stuff that doesn't serve us anymore. The grief and pain of holding on is often more painful than letting go. The experience of personal freedom is in the present moment, and this requires letting go.

Here are some questions you can ask yourself or others to assist in letting go:

What am I truly upset about? What is bothering me?

What am I feeling? Allow those feelings to move through you.

What belief about myself, others, or life do I need to let go of?

What do I truly want for myself?

Whenever you find yourself judging someone and their shortcomings, simply say, "I would *NEVER* ..." Fill in the blank with your judgment, and you will see that you *HAVE* in fact done that before to some degree! For example – "I would *NEVER* say mean things about someone." Most likely you will realize as you say this that you have in fact said mean things about someone before, you simply thought it was deserved. This will assist in the letting go process, in other words letting go of the judgment.

FEELINGS – NOTHING MORE THAN FEELINGS!

"The way you feel shows you who you truly are – the way you act shows others who you are."
Pam Dunn

The *most* important concept here is that **feelings are meant to be felt, not necessarily expressed**. It isn't the expression that helps you move through your feelings, it is the feeling of the feelings.

We waste a lot of time and energy fighting with or judging certain feelings. There are no bad feelings; hurt, anger, sadness are no more bad or good than happy and joy. It is the way we resist and judge our hurt, anger, sadness, fear that makes them seem worse than they are. The benefits of *all* feelings (the truth behind and underneath those feelings) are found in experiencing the feeling.

Most everyone has experienced a broken heart. In other words, we have experienced adverse situations in which we were hurt or saddened. Generally, our automatic reaction to this type of experience is to figure out how it occurred, what caused it, and make sure we know enough to make sure it never occurs again.

This type of process actually *blames* the *feelings* for being the cause of our experience, even if you have worked very hard to take responsibility for your part.

Hearts don't break closed – *HEARTS BREAK OPEN!* So, if you allow yourself to feel the grief, pain, sorrow, hurt from your heart breaking, you will find on the other side an inner strength and depth of compassion that surpasses any type of cynicism.

You must stop being cautious and careful in your life in an effort to avoid certain experiences that may have you feeling something you don't like. Get comfortable with feeling feelings, and discover how they strengthen you. Do this for children, too!

Here is how you *feel* your feelings rather than having to express them. When a situation occurs, you will have an initial feeling. Train yourself to ask, "How am I feeling?" As soon as you have the answer, find out where in your body that feeling originates. Once you notice that place in your body, imagine the feeling traveling down through the bottom of your feet and up through the top of your head. Once you fully experience the feeling throughout your entire body, then you may respond. For example, if I feel angry, I acknowledge the feeling around my sternum. I follow the feeling from there and imagine it moving all the way to my feet. Then I follow the feeling up from there, to my sternum, and up until I imagine it leaving through the top of my head. Now I am free to respond and my response comes from an inner strength, knowing, and authority as well as inner peace.

You can gain a deeper understanding through talking about how you felt about a situation as long as you have felt those feelings first.

Questions to ask yourself or others to identify and feel your feelings:

What am I feeling?

Where in my body do I first feel that feeling?

Once that feeling has moved entirely through my body, how do I want to respond?

ACCEPTANCE – WHAT WILL YOU ACCEPT?

"Trying to 'win' over someone is always a mistake. You stop believing in your worthiness and start hustling for it."
Brene' Brown

Don't accept your shortcomings. Accept your greatness and use that as inspiration to move through overcoming the shortcoming. There is a jargon phrase out there that has become out-dated: "Accept your shortcomings. Accept your faults. That's just the way you are." The meaning is that you should accept yourself wholly—the good *and* the bad. Then there is the philosophy that I operated from starting at a very young age. "Push yourself if you want to get anywhere significant." In other words, I wouldn't do the hard stuff (like study harder) if I took it easy on myself. I thought I needed to be hard on myself. While both of these methods worked to a certain extent, neither one of them made anyone feel great about themselves on the journey. This philosophy did not assist me or anyone in discovering, honoring, or experiencing their innate brilliance or magnificence. The overall purpose was noble, and that's why it's time to update the philosophy.

Don't accept your shortcomings, instead accept your magnificence. Shed lots of light on that brilliance and magnificence, then use that inspiration to help overcome any shortcoming. Use that inspiration to move forward to do whatever may feel hard. Use that inspiration to keep going when you want to quit. Use that inspiration to rise above to become the brilliance and magnificence you know yourself to *be*.

I love to hike. With most good hikes, it involves at least one substantial climb up a hill. At the point when the climb becomes challenging, I know it would not serve me to start telling myself "I can't do this," "It's too hard," "I'll never make it," "I'm not good enough to get up this," "I don't have what it takes," "It doesn't matter," and so on! What gets me through the tough part is letting myself know "I can do this," "I have what it takes," "I'm strong," and so on.

It is the same for our character development. To develop your character, to go beyond your comfort zone, to learn more, inspiration is the key. Teaching ourselves and accepting how magnificent you are will build your character and inspire you to do more.

This is the reality of self-acceptance. We all have a unique magnificence—something, actually many characteristics, that are our gifts. It is innate, and natural, and very positive. Acknowledging them and expressing them gives us the inspiration to tackle anything difficult that we desire to pursue. When you see a bully acting like a bully, imagine them instead operating from their magnificence. Perhaps you see their magnificence as kind or caring or considerate.

So, increase your awareness first by recognizing the ways you beat yourself up and the ways you discourage yourself with the things you say or the things you do. Then begin recognizing all the great things about you. Ask others what they admire about you, find a constant in that. Notice what you do that brings you fulfillment, then see how that translates to an innate quality of yours. Practice every day telling yourself three things you appreciate about yourself that you did that day.

> **Exercise** – Think of three people you admire, then two things you admire about them. Once complete, look over the list and know that if "you spot it, you got it!" You cannot see something in someone else without possessing that quality yourself. Now, decide which qualities you want to bring out in the open.

Focusing on and accepting our shortcomings puts a protective shield around our hearts, and we end up acting out of character (not out of our magnificence) to keep the shield up. Our hearts do not need a shield; that's an outdated limiting belief. An unshielded, unprotected heart is strong, wise and magnificent. It leads the way to the truth of your greatness and provides the fulfillment we all seek. Always remember: it comes from within rather than from outside of us.

You already are that which you have been searching for! It's always been there, you just have to look inside to find it.

Questions to ask yourself and others that will guide you to the acceptance of your magnificence:

> What are 3-5 characteristics that describe my ideal self?
>
> How do I express those characteristics in my daily life?
>
> What is a shortcoming that I would like to eliminate?
>
> What are three steps I can take to transform that shortcoming?

POWER – DO WE REALLY GIVE IT AWAY?

"What gets us into trouble is not what we don't know. It's what we know for sure that just ain't so."
Mark Twain

Power is not taken from you nor is power given away. Your ability to be powerful, feel powerful and express your power always resides within you. Power is used either effectively, ineffectively, or misused. What happens in some difficult instances when you think or feel you've lost your power, is that you have diminished your power with your thoughts, feelings, and beliefs. It means that you have chosen (unconsciously) to withhold your power (to cover it up or put it away). This is what occurs in a victim mindset scenario.

In the case of overpowering, which occurs when acting like a bully, you are misusing your power. While diminishing your power and claiming to be a victim is a covert misuse of power, the bully behavior of overpowering is overt.

Relationships are never about power. You can avoid the will to power over or under in a relationship by choosing to serve. For example: if I am coloring alongside my four year-old niece, I have a choice to serve her by being with her and enjoying coloring together, or I can focus on doing a perfect job of coloring the picture. Love and respect and connection in this scenario represents power. In other words, it is a powerful experience when I am connected with someone in a compassionate and caring way. It is a powerful experience to be loving and respectful in all my interactions.

So, in conclusion, when operating in a bully/victim paradigm you with either be diminishing your ability to be powerful or misusing your power and overpowering. Neither are effective or an expression of magnificence. There are many limiting beliefs about power. The way to express your unlimited power is to believe in yourself and your magnificence, believe in your ability to handle yourself in the best way possible at any time, and believe in the goodness of others.

Questions to ask yourself and others in order to be able to embrace the depth of your power to be, do, or have what you desire:

What are some of the limiting beliefs I have about power?

What belief shall I replace those limiting beliefs with?

Where in my life do I feel so powerful that I don't even need to think about being powerful?

What steps do I need to take to feel powerful in the places I do not feel powerful?

Observe the areas of your life where you are using you power effectively as well as ineffectively.

BOUNDARIES

"Our truest, deepest self is completely free. It is not crippled or compromised by past actions or concerned with identity or status. It comprehends that it has no need to fear the earthly world, and therefore, it has no need to build itself up through fame or wealth or conquest."
Eben Alexander

Setting a boundary is different than putting up a wall. When setting boundaries, it is important to organize yourself around your strengths, not the weaknesses.

For example, one of my sons had a hard time saying "no" to his friends, co-workers, and many others. I am confident many people can relate! Because his weakness is in saying "no," telling him all he needs to do is say "no" to people would seem monumental to him and more challenging, therefore the likelihood of success would be minimized.

Instead of focusing on telling the people in your life "no," it's important to first focus on what you're saying "yes" to. For example, he is asked by his co-workers to go out for drinks after work. He doesn't really want to because his preference was to go to the gym after work. In the past, he would simply skip the gym and go out for drinks, then beat himself up for not going to the gym. Sound familiar? The new way for him is this: when asked to go for drinks when his preference is to go to the gym, he says, "I'm going to the gym tonight right after work, but thanks for asking and let me know next time you go." This way of expression organizes around his strength, which is in saying "Yes!"

PROCESS OF BLAME & ESCAPE FROM BLAME

"You must create your own world. I am responsible for my world."
Louise Nevelson

It is inevitable that at some point we will blame. Blaming is generally ineffective and unfulfilling, however, it is what we resort to when we don't know what else to do. Sometimes the way we recognize we are blaming is by catching ourselves in the act or seeing it after we have done it. Be proactive in discovering ways you blame so you can claim responsibility before blaming. *Here are ways to identify the process of blame:*

1. I increase my awareness of my mistakes and/or shortcomings.
2. I lack the acceptance of my magnificence.
3. I "beat myself up" because I make mistakes.
4. I avoid seeing my faults to get relief from "beating myself up."
5. Since I don't accept my mistakes, I conclude that they must belong to others.
6. I dump my garbage (my problems) into someone else's yard.
7. I start searching for other people's shortcomings and assume that my problems are caused by their shortcomings.
8. I blame others and conclude, "case closed." I stop the investigation and end the search before I discover what I did to cause the problem.
9. I "beat up" other people by judging them because they make mistakes.
10. I counteract the logical intellectual belief of: "I know I am the source of my happiness" by feeling that others are to blame for my unhappiness.
11. I surrender my happiness in the here and now moment in an attempt to show how others are the cause of my problems. I express this in ways that pressures them.
12. Because I overlook how good this moment is, I start concentrating on the future I do not want. I hold a negative vision of the future.

    I combine that vision with worry.

    I enroll others in my negative vision by talking negatively to people.

    This helps to create the very outcome I fear.

13. I get caught in the illusion that other people's mistakes cause my problems.
14. I assume that others have a negative motive. I take on their problems as my own and try to get them to improve.
15. I waste energy feeling I am either getting something I don't deserve, or that I need to pressure others in order to make sure I will get what I do deserve. I blame them for why I do not have it yet.

    I withdraw my ability to influence with statements like:

    "With him, I just can't be heard."

    "It's impossible to get her to change."

    "They just won't listen to me."

    I may avoid doing the things that would influence a change.

    I talk about the problem to people who are not the ones who could change it.
16. I put my energy into pressuring or changing others.
17. The relationship is strained because they don't improve.
18. I attempt to solve the problem by separation, such as:

    I get a separation. I get a divorce. I quit. I fire them. I leave.

    I have an affair. I break up. I leave the organization.
19. I resort to blaming things. For example, I cuss at my tennis racquet to create the feeling that the racquet caused me to miss the shot instead of looking within and seeing that I didn't practice enough.
20. I resort to dividing myself into two parts and blaming myself. Or I confess without accepting the responsibility.

    "I only have myself to blame."

21. I start seeing responsibility as something to be avoided or responsibility as a burden.

22. I start thinking that I have to find just the right person.

    I believe the myth that I must find just the right man or woman to help me feel I am okay or good enough. I believe someone must change something in order for me to be happy, like a partner, boss, child, or sibling.

Discovering the process of blame and escaping from blame is a life-long journey! You will not ever benefit from believing that you have conquered your blaming and that you are wrong, bad or justified in blaming. You will understand the value of eliminating the bully/victim paradigm when you know that it is a process of discovering that you are blaming, then taking responsibility for expressing and acting from your magnificence in order to escape from blame.

Here are some points to assist you in the escape from blame:

1. Monitor my tone of voice to recognize when I'm not looking within for solutions.
2. Monitor my serenity to see when I am blaming or claiming to be a victim and out of balance.
3. Assume that my difficulties are caused by my mistakes or my actions.
4. Assume that others have positive intentions for me.
5. When feeling hurt, look within to discover the original hurt and limiting belief. Or, look to see where I am fishing for something rather than asking directly.
6. Work to stop pressuring and judging other people and myself.

7. Stop talking about the mistakes other people make; focus on their magnificence.
8. Monitor when I create feelings that create the illusion that others are causing my problems.
9. Ask myself, "What am I afraid of?"
10. Look within and ask, "What is it that I am unaware of that I may not want to see about myself?"
11. Recognize that I always have the capacity to get what I deserve. Avoid putting energy into proving that I don't deserve it, or that I can't get what I deserve.
12. Strive for steady improvement, giving myself plenty of time.
13. Instead of saying, "What is wrong with me?" ask, "What do I need to change about the way I am managing my life in order to improve?"
14. Give myself permission to have some shortcomings that I will never change.
15. Don't assume I should have already evolved to the point where I know how to love unconditionally. Recognize that I am in this life to learn how to do that.
16. Practice becoming more tolerant of others.
17. Be more comfortable with myself. Laugh at my mistakes. See them as smiles.
18. Look for what is beautiful in this moment.
19. Recognize when I am dwelling on a future I don't want, and replace those thoughts with a vision of a magnificent future.

20. Look and listen to examine where people's criticism about me is accurate and do that through the lens of my magnificence.

21. When I feel I should forgive someone, ask myself, "What do they need to forgive me for?"

22. After looking inside to recognize my mistakes, look deeper to see the beautiful purpose for my behavior.

23. Start seeing responsibility, my ability to respond, as the key to reclaiming my ability to influence.

Trusting things will turn out well does not influence that outcome. Trust in yourself and your ability to take actions that will make them turn out the way you want. We are much wiser than we think.

> **Practice** – When you meditate (hopefully everyday), send love to those you love and care about and to those you judge!
>
> Pick one process of blame and/or one escape from blame per week and work with and through them.

Life is a reflection - look for the BEAUTY!

"Our first act as free men was to throw ourselves onto the provisions. Not of revenge. And even when we were no longer hungry, there was still no one who thought of revenge."

ELIE WIESEL
from *Night*

CHAPTER 9

COMPONENTS IN THE PARADIGM OF MAGNIFICENCE

Once you've gained an initial understanding and had some successes through practice, you'll be able to experience the power of additional components that will guide you farther down the path of changing the paradigm of bully/victim to the paradigm of magnificence!

EMPATHY

"Empathy is not merely a basic principle. It is also the only path by which one can reach the truth about life and society."
Unknown

There are so many different viewpoints about empathy. So let's talk about empathy in the context of eliminating the bully/victim paradigm. When someone feels like a victim, it's important to acknowledge their hurt, sorrow, etc., while empathizing with their magnificence. In other words, you see them greater than they see themselves in that moment. It doesn't mean you should preach to them, or try to convince them they are greater than they see themselves in that moment. It means you can acknowledge pain while seeing their magnificence at the same time.

Dr. Daniel Goleman, author of the bestseller, *Emotional Intelligence*, states, "Leaders with empathy do more than sympathize with people around them: they use their knowledge to improve their companies in subtle, but important ways." This doesn't mean that they agree with everyone's view or try to please everybody. Rather, they "thoughtfully consider" employees' feelings (along with other factors) in the process of making intelligent decisions. Even if empathy doesn't come naturally to some of us, I believe that we can develop this capacity."

I quote a business perspective because in the moment you are faced with someone feeling like a victim, you are in a position to step up as the leader.

As stated by Dr. Goleman above, all beings have the ability to develop the capacity to be empathetic. So it will take understanding a human being's basic needs.

As we learned earlier, all human beings have the same four basic needs. They are:

To be loved/cared about

To be powerful

To be valuable

To belong

These four basic needs take place inside of the relationship and its interactions rather than in what you say. In other words, actions speak louder than words. When doing this you are seeing people and yourself as having those needs met and seeing them and yourself as confident in those ways of being.

When you see someone operating from bully behavior, it is vitally important to be empathetic. The key is to *be*, not to *do* empathy. Being empathetic assures you are genuine and doing your best to understand them rather than doing something to get them to stop doing something! Being empathetic does not allow for assumptions either. Don't try to assume what may be going on. *Be* with them and listen. Maybe ask questions or seek to find out, and you will help them discover their magnificence beyond the pain and anger.

If you think this seems like a daunting possibility, I can make it easier and simpler for you. *Being* empathetic with others will become easier the better you become at being empathetic, understanding, loving, and friendly with yourself. In other words, learn to eliminate bullying for yourself with your thoughts and self-talk, *and* learn to be continuously responsible for all your responses, especially when you feel like a victim. If you *really* want to live a life expressing your magnificence, you must begin by learning and talking about what is in the way.

Empathy Exercise - when you receive a complaint from someone that you would like to resolve, practice either one of the following formats:

"When I ...
Repeat their complaint in their words, then say,

like I did ...
State an example of when you did it.

I must make you feel ..."
Feel the feelings while you are saying this. Deeply empathize. Do not explain why you did what they accused you of doing. Do not justify doing it. Just empathize as much as possible. Do not say you are sorry. Make sure your partner feels heard, understood, and feels like his complaint was a valid complaint.

OR

"I understand ... (repeat their exact words).
Empathize with what they are feeling, and you may tell them those feelings.

Take responsibility.
Listen and watch for when they feel heard and know that you understand their viewpoint.

Continue conversing until this has been accomplished.
Be sure you are not making excuses or apologizing.
Be sure you only make promises you are willing to keep.

TENDERNESS = REVERENCE

"What comes from the heart, goes to the heart."
Samuel Coleridge

Sometimes we confuse tenderness with being gentle. While they seem to be interchangeable, most of the time when we refer to gentleness it is because we are trying not to be its opposite.

Everyone (even the bully) is capable of tenderness. To be tender or to allow that tenderness to be seen, requires vulnerability. When I say vulnerable, I mean open-hearted. Tenderness and open-hearted are the same. In order to allow yourself to be seen that way or to express that for yourself, you must treat yourself and others with reverence. When there is no reverence for oneself or others, you will slip into the bully/victim paradigm.

What truly heals is tenderness and gratitude for that tenderness. Rather than trying to save the world or ourselves, we wonder how we are doing or how other people are doing, and reflect on how our actions and judgments affect other people.

> **Practice** – Every time you catch yourself judging someone, stop immediately and tell yourself three things you love and appreciate about them. Feel the tenderness (the softness of your heart) return.

NOT CAUTIOUS, NOT CAREFUL – BUT FULL OF CARE.

"You never know until you try to reach them how accessible men are; but you must approach each man by the right door."
Henry Ward Beecher

Our hearts and other people's hearts do not need to be treated carefully or gently. If we honor the reverence of a heart's tenderness, we will be full of care with ourselves and others in terms of the way we treat ourselves and others. By full of care, I mean that rather than act carefully, operate as someone that cares, or is full of care. Hearts are not fragile; egos are fragile!

There is no need to be cautious or careful with yourself; be full of care. Being full of care means you begin with knowing that their negative behavior is not a reflection of who they truly are. Being full of care is seeing them greater than they are acting in that moment. If someone is acting like a bully, being cautious or careful with them will indicate to them that you are afraid. Being afraid around someone acting like a bully is basically telling them that they are dangerous. Most people acting like bullies are not necessarily dangerous, but they are not full of care. If you give what you want (like care) then you may be able to disarm them, but at the very least you will not match their behavior.

Suffering, anger, and hopelessness all appear in your life when you practice and live from seeing people as mean or nice, good or bad, right or wrong. Practice eliminating that paradigm by caring more about people and going beyond that to being full of care for people.

> **Practice** - Remove "I don't care," "I could care less," and other types of phrases from your vocabulary of conversations. Do random acts of caring kindness.

MISTAKES

"Learning from your mistakes is the great equalizer of regret."
Drew Dunn

Most of us grew up deciding that we needed to either not make any mistakes or be gentle with ourselves when we do make a mistake. Think about it. What occurred for you that had you decide that? For me, in school, there were lots of red checks and focusing on what was wrong rather what was right. For others, they may have been punished or berated or had love withdrawn when they made a mistake. Even if that was unintentional, the limiting belief begins and remains.

This is why I love Drew's quote. Mistakes are meant to be learning opportunities, not a chance to validate your current limitations or an opportunity to beat yourself or others up. The key is to discover a way to learn from the mistake without first feeling like you should cover it up or make excuses for it.

If you take on the responsibility of knowing your magnificence, then when you do make a mistake you will immediately discover what is to be learned. Another tip is to become *comfortable* with mistakes. When you realize you have made a mistake, imagine sitting in a big comfy chair. Imagine that now! Can you see how you feel relaxed throughout your body? If you stay in the comfy chair with that relaxed feeling, you will open up to discover what can be learned from the mistake.

> **Practice** – Consider practicing with a friend. Take turns sharing some mistakes you have made (that you previously judged) and imagine you are in the comfy chair!
>
> Practice non-judgment with mistakes.

BROKEN HEARTS HAVE NEEDS.

"Between right and wrong doing there is a field, I will meet you there."
Rumi

A broken heart is an open heart. Hearts break open, not closed. When our heart is broken it is the time to nurture that tender heart with reverence. When our heart is broken it is the time to be full of care. Judging, blaming, focusing on the how you were wronged is what shuts your heart down.

Regret can help you to remember to not do the same things again. Shame makes you forget who you are. Guilt helps you realize there is a place you haven't been fully responsible yet. "Wise men often feel regret. Fools wallow in their sorrow. The former helps you to forget, the latter destroys tomorrow."

Life is not a performance. Life is an experience. That means some experiences are heart-opening, some are heart-closing, some are heart-breaking – all are something that makes us who we are. Finding meaning in the face of the adversity or experience makes whatever occurs within our heart worthwhile. That doesn't mean you find meaning with the adversity. For example, any family that's lost someone as a result of being bullied does not need to find meaning *in the adversity*; they can find meaning in their lives *as a result of the adversity*. That provides a legacy for their loved one.

Have you ever noticed that once you have had your heart broken, you tend to be cautious and careful? That need seems justified as a caring protective measure. Life and people are unpredictable, so it's important to know what you need to feel safe to open your heart. When we say things like, "I don't feel safe opening my heart with you," we relate to a feeling and yet associate safety with something physical. It is important to identify that what you really need is *emotional* safety. Seek to know yourself well enough to recognize what the people in your life do that makes you feel emotionally safe and what they do that makes you feel emotionally unsafe. For example, when I was young and I was upset about something that happened with a friend, I would share with one of my other friends who would laugh or say something sarcastic. This was really my friend showing me their discomfort and at the same time wanting to help me feel better, but I shut down and then became cautious because I believed that if I share vulnerably, I would be laughed at. Clearly a limited way of thinking!

Experiences like the one above are not reasons to not share vulnerably or to claim that it is not safe to share. Experiences like that are opportunities to learn who you want to share your vulnerability with and when.

> **Practice** - Next time you feel vulnerable, be very loving to yourself, and then find someone to share with; asking them to only listen.

JUDGMENT VS. CONCERN

"For me, it is possible to have the greatest care and concern for someone and bench, suspend, or even remove him from the team."
Coach John Wooden

Judgment will always counteract the vulnerability of concern. Let me explain with a story about my friend and her husband. Jennifer and Paul are married with two children. They are in the process of adding on to their home, hiring architects, contractors, builders, etc. Jennifer was asking Paul about the finances of the upcoming changes. She didn't understand a few things and suddenly became concerned by something Paul said.

Immediately Jennifer began expressing her concern because, as she said, "things always seem to end up this way" when they have conversations about money. Paul was instantly defensive and retaliated by telling Jennifer he couldn't find a way to talk to her when she was "like that." As you can imagine, the remainder of the conversation and the evening was dampened. And they never really talked about the original question or concern. If you think about it, this scenario is often typical of conversations when a concern is being communicated. Here is why: When the concern is laced with judgment, the vulnerability behind the original question that is causing the concern is not communicated. It gets lost and unfortunately the judgment is the only thing that's felt and reacted to.

> **Practice** – When you are genuinely concerned about something, it is important to check in with yourself and allow your heart to open to the vulnerability of that concern. Communicate from there rather than protecting yourself with judgment.

SUPPORT - WE ALL NEED AND WANT IT!

"No person is your friend who demands your silence, or denies your right to grow."
Alice Walker

Support is a word that has so many meanings and judgments attached to it. In some cases we believe we're owed support and that we shouldn't have to ask for it, especially from our loved ones.

We think they should just know that we need it and how to support us! Most of us don't feel comfortable or justified in asking for support. And many of us believe support means only positive comments and helpful actions. This is only a small portion of what support really means.

It isn't supportive to the person acting like a bully to accept their behavior or only to punish them. Similarly it would not be supportive of someone operating from a victim mindset to continue making it alright for them to feel that way about themselves. There's a question you can always ask yourself to check-in with how to support someone: What will support their magnificence? So it will help a lot if you to know what support looks and feels like for *you*.

When I facilitate our weekend programs there is always a group of volunteer staff. I always let them know that the best way they can support me is to be accountable to their assigned jobs, and when I ask them to do something, they do it! In the end, I have held them accountable to their magnificence because they commit to serve the participants through doing their assigned jobs and many other things. I also know that I feel supported by encouraging words especially when I have just taken a risk. In those moments, I always ask someone I love to support me by encouraging me by sharing something they saw me do well during that risk.

When you communicate your way of wanting to be supported, you give someone the opportunity to serve. You get supported (which feels great), and they get to serve (which feels great)!

> **Practice** – Discover how you want to be supported, and share how you like to be supported with someone.

COMPASSION

"If you allow life to show you yourself in new ways, so that you may know yourself in those ways, AND you reconcile within yourself that which life has shown you, THEN you become compassion."
Gregg Braden

I love that Gregg Braden has created a science to compassion. It makes it more accessible and appealing. Compassion is the combination of so many ways of being; it is an evolved and enlightened concept and can only be achieved when you have put *your* issues and beliefs aside for the purpose of relating to others. Braden says, "The science of compassion allows the witnessing/experience of an event without the polarized judgment as to the rightness or wrongness of the event."

Compassion is a way of being, because it involves feelings, thoughts, and actions. To be compassionate with the person acting like a bully is to see him or her being magnificent, recognize the bully behavior, and help them take a step toward their magnificence, knowing they have what it takes to take the adventure to magnificence. To be compassionate with the person operating from a victim mindset is to see him or her as magnificently powerful, while at the same time seeing them claiming to be a victim and help them take a step toward magnificence, knowing they have what it takes to take that step even if they don't see the end yet.

Pema Chodron says, "In cultivating compassion we draw from the wholeness of our experience—our suffering, our empathy, as well as our cruelty and terror. It has to be this way. Compassion is not a relationship between the healer and the wounded. It is a relationship between equals."

And Brene' Brown, in *Gifts of Imperfection*, says it so clearly: "We have to stay away from convincing ourselves that we hate someone, or that they deserve to feel bad, so that we can feel better about holding them accountable. That's where we get into trouble; when we talk ourselves into disliking someone so we're more comfortable holding them accountable. We're simply priming ourselves for the shame and blame game. It is impossible to practice compassion from a place of resentment."

> Practice – Read Gregg Braden's book, *Walking Between the Worlds: The Science of Compassion*. Read Brene' Brown's book, *The Gifts of Imperfection*. Both of these books have the most effective explanations and ways of being compassion.

IT IS ALWAYS YOUR CHOICE!

THE WOLVES WITHIN

by David Griffith

An old grandfather, whose grandson came to him with anger at a schoolmate who had done him injustice said, "Let me tell you a story."

It is as if there are two wolves inside me; one is good and does no harm. He lives in harmony with those around him and does not take offense when no offense was intended. He will only fight when it is right to do so, and without discouraging others.

But the other wolf, ah! He is full of anger. The littlest thing will set him into a fit of temper. He fights and discourages. He cannot think clearly because of his anger. It is hard to live with these two wolves inside me, for both of them try to dominate my Spirit.

The boy looked intently into his grandfather's eyes and asked, "Which one wins, grandfather?" The grandfather solemnly answered, "The one I feed."

It is truly always your choice to feed the belief and feeling that serves your magnificence or not.

I remember when I first began embarking on the dream of doing workshops to deliver messages like this one, I did a two-hour workshop on forgiveness. It was well-attended; there were forty-five people there. I fully immersed myself and really enjoyed every minute of it. Upon completion, I handed out an evaluation form and asked them to give it to me completed on their way out.

Out of forty-five evaluations, two of them were not favorable and forty-three were excellent. I spent hours dwelling on the two negative forms, discouraging myself from ever doing it again! Suddenly, I had an awakening and realized what I was doing; what I was feeding! I began encouraging myself immediately.

> **Practice** - If your thoughts are rapidly invalidating your magnificence, ask yourself "What do I want to feel right now about this?" Once you decide, ask yourself immediately, "What thoughts do I need to think in order to feel this way?"
>
> Every morning tell yourself three things you love about yourself. Every evening tell yourself three things that you appreciate about yourself from that day.

"YES" IS A CORE VALUE!

"It is better to light a candle than to curse the darkness."
Chinese Proverb

Every time we say "no" it goes against an innate core value—the core value that says how in some way we all desire to serve, be helpful, be valuable, care about others, and so on. So, to say "no" goes against all of those things. When you say "no", know what you are saying "yes" to?

The same goes for being against anything or anyone. To protest something is the same concept. To protest or be against anything means we are fighting. While we may be able to justify the fight, it goes against our core values: to be loved, to be powerful, to be valuable and to belong. So what to do? When saying "no" be very conscious of what you are saying "yes" to. When you are against something, switch your focus to what you are "for" or what you support. Against war, for peace and cooperation, for example.

Stop being helpful by making sure you are saying "yes" to your desires and service. Most of us were taught how important it is to be helpful. We praise, adore, and look up to those we have decided are helpful. Let me say, first of all, this isn't wrong or really a problem. But there is a bit of a problem that comes from this belief. People start asking themselves *before* doing anything if their service would be helpful to others. This becomes a problem because you begin to do things for others, but your motive shifts, and you begin to ask yourself, "how can *I* be good **like** Gandhi, Mother Theresa, the Dalai Lama" or anyone you admire? While what you do may be helpful, the other people don't get that intention because the intention is about *you impressing* them or you being like someone else!

So, while all the above people have been helpful, they had an original motive that had nothing to do with helping. They were doing what *they* desired. They were in service to their magnificence. So spare everyone and stop being so helpful. Instead, start doing what you desire! I am absolutely sure it will serve others in some way and frankly, unless I come right out and ask you to help me in a certain way, you are only guessing if it would be helpful or not. In some ways being helpful means that you put yourself above the person you are helping. Remember this about the intention.

There is profound fulfillment when I am going about the activity of doing my heart's desire and someone shares with me how helpful I was to them. It is a validation of how valuable living from my heart's desire is, and it shines my light, my magnificence ever brighter.

> **Practice** – Do something that serves your magnificence today and then notice how it served others. Review the Commitment Chart.

Mom – matriarch, mentor, role-model, friend—all around an amazing woman that leads her family with love.

IN CONCLUSION

It takes a lot of courage, a lot of love, and a lot of compassion to see the perceived bully as greater than their actions. Each and every one of you have that ability. It takes a lot of strength, a lot of faith, and a lot of compassion to see the perceived victim as greater than their beliefs. Each and every one of you have that ability.

It is critical to rise to this challenge because it is your way to stop adding anger, revenge, depression and discouragement to the world, and replace that with the ability to treat each other and ourselves more compassionately, see ourselves and others as brilliant, judge from the beauty, and care about the pain. This is the richness the world and you deserve to experience.

So, how do you meet these challenges—a perceived bully/victim situation, and see everyone from the perspective of magnificence? You have the power to do this, to create this. It is time to look inside!

Viktor Frankl said - "*I have come to the conclusion that I am the decisive element. I possess tremendous power to make life miserable or joyous. I can be a tool of torture or an instrument of inspiration. I can humiliate or humor, hurt or heal. In all situations it is my response that decides whether a crisis is elevated.*"

There is *far* more to the bully, the victim, and their behavior that lies beneath the way they *act*. It is time to move beyond our limiting paradigm, and begin seeing ourselves and others as magnificent beings that may *act* mean from time to time. Acting mean is not an indicator of being mean. So decide who you want to be, and learn about yourself, especially when you are *not* operating that way, and then go on to discover, honor and express your magnificence—assist others to do that too!

Embarking on a new dream takes a lot of support.

RESOURCES

Your Infinite Life Training & Coaching Company – coaching, blogs, mentorships, classes – www.YourInfiniteLifeOnline.com

Indigo Village Educational Foundation – resources for parenting, books, parenting classes – www.IndigoVillage.com

www.PeaceInYourHome.com – online resources for parenting, personal development and nutrition

www.DrTimJordan.com – online resources and books

www.CampWeloki.com – camps and enriching weekends for kids and teens

www.WholeHeartedParenting.com – parenting classes, personal development programs, blogs and articles

www.DSivils.com – guiding your life to purpose through coaching and guided quests

www.VillageGateAcademy.com - an alternative school for kids K-8th grade

For more ideas on good books for self development, parenting, spiritual development, alternative schools, etc., contact me at info@yourinfinitelifeonline.com

ABOUT YOUR INFINITE LIFE TRAINING & COACHING COMPANY

Our mission is to assist people to discover, honor, and express their unique contribution in the world—their magnificence. We serve as a bridge to assist you, and give you tools to discover, honor, and express your unique contribution in the world—your magnificence.

THE REMEMBRANCE COURSE - A MAGNIFICENCE EXPERIENCE

Remember a time when you felt magnificent? Remember a time when you responded from the expression of your brilliance? At The Remembrance Course, you will be given the time to focus on yourself, and discover competencies and gifts within yourself that will assist you in getting what you most desire from life by way of unleashing your innate magnificence. You will develop the courage and insight to take the steps (or leaps) by becoming aware of limiting beliefs you have been operating from that have unknowingly been preventing you from seeing yourself through your greater vision. Once you are aware of the limiting beliefs, you will form new ones along with ideas and choices to achieve your greater goals. The Remembrance Course - A Magnificence Experience provides accelerated pathways to help you more easily and quickly gain positive insight, arrive at new conclusions, and take new actions, leading to greater ease and effectiveness in achieving your goals.

FREEDOM TO BE - AN EMBRACING LIFE EXPERIENCE

The training provides you with tools to feel and act based upon your stated values. You will also learn and practice unique ways of being empathetic to others, by learning the process of blame, how to let go of blaming, and to knowing what to do when you are being blamed. You will discover how to be even more self-reliant and to release self-imposed limitations including at times when you feel like a victim. By becoming acutely aware of what underlies your actions, you can become comfortable with all aspects of yourself and of others, which allows you to see yourself and others truthfully and with great compassion. By connecting with your deepest intentions to love and be loved you will experience a new sense of freedom and power to create the relationships you desire.

PERSONAL & EXECUTIVE COACHING SESSIONS

These sessions are designed for those who want to integrate and expand on the experiences and understandings they already have, as well as explore new possibilities with confidence. The sessions are particularly helpful if you are experiencing new challenges or current changes happening in your life or would like to create more confidence in your pursuit to create some changes for yourself.

INQUIRE ABOUT ADDITIONAL TRAININGS:

The Quest Retreat
Advanced Level Mastery Training
Coach Certification Training
Instructor Certification Training
Mastery Mentorship Training

PURCHASE LAMINATED POSTERS INDIVIDUALLY FOR $22 EACH

(choose either 16x20 or 24x36)

- Levels of Commitment Chart
- Self Reliance vs. Victim Mindset Chart
- Various Tones & Turnarounds Chart
- Limiting Belief Cycle of Creation & Eliminations Chart
- Conflict Resolution Communication Model

You can purchase the posters and more books directly at www.YourInfiniteLifeOnline.com. Books may also be purchased at www.BalboaPress.com.

BIBLIOGRAPHY

How Children Succeed - Paul Tough

Man's Search for Meaning - Viktor Frankl

The Gifts of Imperfection - Brene' Brown

When Things Fall Apart - Pema Chodron

The Servant - James Hunter

Walking Between the Worlds - Gregg Braden

Emotional Intelligence - Daniel Goleman

Love living life! Bryant Park, NY in November.

ABOUT THE AUTHOR

PAMELA DUNN has been a catalyst for transformative learning for more than twenty years. Her dynamic approach to training and development stems from her innate belief that each and every person is magnificent and has a unique gift to contribute. It is Pam's belief that given the right atmosphere, everyone can discover, honor, and express their unique contribution in the world with the intention of unleashing their magnificence. Once magnificence is unleashed, one can express themselves in a self-reliant, interdependent manner, thus benefiting not only the individual, but their family, workplace, and community as well.

Ms. Dunn has taught and lectured throughout the United States and Europe within corporations, schools, sports teams, government agencies, and private organizations. Pam's ability to get to the root of a situation or challenge, with grace and reverence for those she works with, provides an unparalleled environment for growth and change. Pam's previous corporate background in the area of executive development with experience in banking, service, retail, and sports teams & coaches has provided her with a solid understanding of existing environments and an uncanny ability to gain agreement and buy-in from those she works with.

Pamela resides in St. Louis, MO when not traveling. Her three grown sons and a new daughter-in-law are expressing their magnificent selves in different places in the world.